KotecKi

MW00331676

PR: A Personal Record of Running from Anorexia

By Amber Sayer

"PR: A Personal Record of Running from Anorexia," by Amber Sayer. ISBN 978-1-62137-243-1 (Softcover) 978-1-62137-244-8 (Ebook).

Published 2013 by Virtualbookworm.com Publishing Inc., P.O. Box 9949, College Station, TX 77842, US. ©2013, Amber Sayer. All rights reserved. No part of this publication may be reproduced, stored in a retrieval system, or transmitted in any form or by any means, electronic, mechanical, recording or otherwise, without the prior written permission of Amber Sayer.

Manufactured in the United States of America.

Foreword

I DECIDED TO WRITE this memoir after an article by Barry Bearak appeared in the *New York Times* called "Young Endurance Runners Draw Cheers and Concerns," [4] about 10- and 12-year-old sisters who compete in endurance races as long as 13+ miles. While the article was not directly about the problems I had been wanting to bring to the fore, it seemed like a good starting point. I had been tossing around the goal for some time of writing about my personal struggle with anorexia and distance running. I felt like I was not emotionally strong enough to conjure up such painful memories, and I also worried – and still do – that my honesty would reveal things that would upset my family, friends, and others.

This memoir chronicles my entry into the world of elite young female distance runners and my battle with long-term, severe anorexia. In many ways, the two fed into one another. I developed into a pretty good runner quickly, and then became quite successful. Unfortunately, as a ten-year-old girl, I developed an eating disorder, which was exacerbated when I began running competitively at the age of twelve. In many ways, running fueled my eating disorder – the faster I ran, the less I wanted to eat, and the more I wanted to run. Female runners' performance tends to improve with reduced body fat, and as my disease progressed through the end of my junior year of high school, my running improved – I won several state championships, a New England Championship, and placed 2nd and 4th in two major National Championships.

I have worked in the fitness industry for the past seven years. It is impossible, even without my background in exercise physiology and nutrition, to be unaware of the obesity epidemic and the increasing number of sedentary children. I believe sports and fitness are great for children. Besides being good for their health, sports teach teamwork, goal setting, challenges and triumphs, patience, and the value of hard work. They give kids a sense of pride and confidence. All that said, I think there are an increasing number of young children these days that are doing too much, too soon. Kids are specializing in sports at young ages, which can lead to overtraining injuries and burnout. I know of a 12-year old lacrosse player who has already suffered three concussions, and a young soccer player who has already torn her ACL twice.

When I finally started overcoming my eating disorder, I was in my senior year of high school, trying to figure out where to go to college. The trouble was, I didn't know what I wanted. Running and eating (or lack thereof) had consumed most of the previous eight years. I struggled with my decision and chose a highly competitive DI school, which was an unhealthy fit at the time. I transferred schools after one year. Even worse, I had immense difficulty running because once I became a healthy weight, my body wasn't used to carrying any weight and I was slow, fragile, and unbelievably susceptible to injury.

One of my motivations to write this memoir stems from my desire to help prevent runners from being in my situation – a broken-down body, memories of greatness, pain from the loss of that greatness, a missed childhood, isolation, loneliness, and damage to relationships. I see photos of the top runners at my former high school, pictures in the newspaper from the State Championships I used to run in, and other images of "running sensations" that circulate on the Internet, and they all look the same to me: dangerously thin. Do they all have eating disorders? Maybe not. Do they all restrict their calories and/or run too much? Probably. As someone who's been there, I feel so compelled to do something to try and stop them, to shake some sense into them, to shine light on a problem that's obvious, yet overlooked. I have to at least try, even at the risk of upsetting the people that I love. I cringe at the sight of photos of myself during my thinnest days in disbelief at what I did to my body – and yet, a small piece of me will always miss running in the spotlight and racing at such a high level that I was untouchable. Why do females have to be so thin to be great?

It's not all bad. While my affliction with anorexia has been an incredibly tough battle for me to fight, running has provided me with many of the best opportunities of my life and shaped who I am today. I try to live my life without regrets. While I can't say I regret running so much when I was younger, I am very aware of the physical and emotional consequences I still deal with today.

My hope is that my experience with anorexia and the pursuit of distance running at an elite level, while unique in some ways, can be used as a tool for athletes, coaches, parents, friends, teammates, and peers to help address the pervasive issue of eating disorders in young female distance runners and other athletes. I am very proud of the records I hold from high school and my running performances, but truthfully, I am more proud of my ability to overcome such a severe disease. In Amherst, Massachusetts, my name is linked to records on athletic plaques displayed in the hallway of my former high school, and I'm sure my times are used by girls - not much unlike myself - who are on the team working to improve their running. While I'm glad the good parts – the fast times, the big smile, and the love of the sport – are remembered fondly, I want girls to understand all the bad that came with that – both for me then, and that I will carry with me my whole life.

Michael Caine once said, "Be like a duck. Calm on the surface, but paddling like the dickens underneath." The underneath – the unhealthy desire to remain so lean that I would be fast – is the part I never talked about. I feel guilty that as a role model for female runners, especially in my hometown, I was not healthy. My goal is to try to improve the value of my legacy by breathing truth into the struggles I faced, to try to influence others to be healthy first, and fast second.

Dedication

I DEDICATE THIS BOOK to my family – for sticking with me during the disease, for seeing past the mistakes I made and the lies I told, and for giving me a chance to be a better, stronger adult. To my friends and teammates who stood by my side through the ups and downs, and to the ones I lost and hurt on the journey – I am deeply sorry. To Arthur Keene, Christopher Gould, Alison Wade, and Julie LaFreniere – the best coaches. To all the people who supported me then and now. To everyone battling the disease - may you find the strength and courage to break free with the love and support of your community. And to Ben, the best friend and husband I could ever ask for. You have taught me that our interests do not define us. We are defined by our personality, our passion, and by the way we lead our lives.

ON A MUGGY MORNING in July 2002, I watched my sister, Emily, pull out of the driveway and head to work. I took the stairs two at a time to my bedroom and threw on a tank top and running shorts. My heart was racing; I was in a frenzied panic to get out the door running. My parents were both at work, and Emily would be gone for a few hours. My running shoes still felt warm and damp from the four-mile run I'd completed just three hours prior.

It was the summer between my sophomore and junior years of high school. I had already completed my "run" for the day, under the watchful eyes of my family. This second run was my run, my time. I zeroed out my watch and trotted down the driveway, my legs still slightly stiff from pushing through the morning run as fast as possible. After all, I was only allowed to run thirty minutes per day. I had to go as fast as possible to maximize the number of miles I could fit in.

With the swiftness of gazelle, I flew down the street toward the center of town, about to embark in my new favorite route – a solid ten-mile course that took me through some quiet roads in my hometown. The sun was nearing its maximum height, and the heat bounced off the pavement in visible blurry ripples. I didn't mind. *Just push, Am. Let's be a champ today.*

The run was unremarkable as far as my training was concerned. It had recently become typical for me to complete two runs before noon. Nearly effortlessly, I cranked out the ten miles in just under seventy minutes, panting and slowing my pace to a staggered walk when I reached our driveway. My face was beet red. *It's a scorcher today.* The screen door slammed behind me as I entered my quiet home. With my sneakers still on, I carelessly tracked mud on the kitchen floor as I walked over to the sink. I gulped down three big glasses of water, and then took the sponge and cleaned up my dirty footprints.

I went upstairs to my bedroom to undress and jump in the shower, when I saw the scale next to my bureau. *I better weigh myself. Mom's going to check me tomorrow.* My clothes and shoes were saturated with sweat and I was starting to feel dizzy. I tapped the scale with my foot: 0.0. Then I stepped on. The five-second deliberation time for my weight to be reported seemed to stretch on forever. 68.0. *68 pounds in clothes and shoes?!* I stared at the number in disbelief. *Uh oh.* Even in the depths of my anorexia, I knew that was too low. I thought I was still at least 75 pounds, and my parents thought I was in the low 80s. I took off my shoes and my running clothes and went down the hall to our laundry hamper to bury them near the bottom, hiding the evidence of my clandestine run. Then I got in the shower.

Lying in my bed awake that night, I peeked under the covers at my skeletal body. *God, help me.* And yet like every other day, when morning came, my mind resumed its obsession with consuming as little food as possible and running as much as I could.

1.
"The Happiest Girl in the World"

AS A CHILD, I was nicknamed "the happiest girl in the world," and
I was, due to my endless energy, a supportive family that provided
me with everything I needed, and self-confidence that could not be
shattered. Every week I had a different dream, and I imagined all
of them possible.

My parents described me as a fun-loving ball of energy,
curious about the world with love for everything and everyone. I
was very hyperactive, intelligent, and sweet. I loved to learn, to
play, to be outside, and to spend time with the family. I also
enjoyed tinkering with "inventions," working at my arts and crafts
table to make dioramas, origami creations, dollhouses out of
cardboard boxes and sponges, or anything imaginable and
unimaginable with pipe cleaners, felt, clay, glitter, and junk my
mom would give me. I liked to disassemble electronics to
investigate how they worked, and pretend to be a detective and
wander around the house trying to solve "mysteries."

I was also very resourceful. In our household, my parents
taught us to make our own fun, to create something out of
nothing, and that we weren't going to spend a lot of money on
things we didn't absolutely need. We were not particularly poor
when I was young, but I was the youngest of three girls and my
mom only worked part-time as an aerobics instructor until I was
six years old. She had taken time off from mental health nursing
to raise my sisters and me. My parents had no money when they
first started dating. They grew from nothing – a couple on food
stamps that used a cardboard box as a kitchen table. I believe this
taught them to spend very wisely, watch income and expenses, and
that happiness does not necessarily come from money.

You can do plenty without spending much. We clipped coupons on Sunday nights and sorted them by food type in a blue index card box that was stored prominently in the kitchen. Friday nights, we gathered around the table scouring the classified ads for the garage sales the next morning. We circled the ads that sounded promising for things my mom needed for the house, and then planned our route to ensure that we would hit the "biggest" sales first before the good stuff sold. We got all of our clothes from our older cousin, who passed them to Ashleigh (my oldest sister), then Emily, and finally to me. Tag sales, the Salvation Army, or the secondhand clothing store in the center of our town, Amherst, Massachusetts, were the only places we ever purchased clothing.

This mentality encouraged my sisters and me to play very creatively when we were young. Until I was five years old, I grew up in an old farmhouse in Brookline, New Hampshire – one of the least populated towns in the state. My sisters and I invented games such as "Old Friend." I was the "old friend" and my two sisters were the "new friends." My job was to scavenge our yard and gardens for various "requests" while they sat up in the tree. Then they would lower a pail on a rope to me. I would fill it with the goods, and they would reel it up, sending me on my way for another bucketful. I'd run around gathering strawberries, snap peas, or sometimes just acorns to give to the "new friends." It certainly sounds sad in retrospect, but at the time, I just felt happy to have a role in the game and content that I was outside playing.

It wasn't until I was in elementary school that it became apparent to me that I did not always have what other kids seemed to. For instance, the first pairs of new store-bought pants my parents ever bought for me were two pairs we got at the Gap on vacation, right before I started seventh grade. I was so excited about the pairs of my brand-new pants that I saved the price tags and taped them in my journal with an arrow that said "New REAL pants!!" I proudly wore one of the pairs to school on the first day of seventh grade. A popular girl from my elementary school said, "Eww. You wear cargo pants? Those are for boys!" Man, was my self-esteem rattled. I kept my hands plastered at my sides the rest of the day to try and cover the pockets that fell mid-way down the leg.

I was also self-conscious about my food in elementary school. My mom never bought packaged snacks or boxed cereals. She made her own vats of healthy granola for us that we kept in the freezer. A typical snack for school was a small chunk of mozzarella cheese off the block, smashed into cling wrap - a mock string cheese. Girl Scout Cookies were the only exception for packaged "regular" food that we had, because we were very involved in Girl Scouting - even my father was part of the troop. Kids in elementary school love to trade food. No one would ever trade with me. One time, I managed to trade Girl Scout Cookies for a Fruit Roll-Up. Why I saw that trade as a big victory on my end blows my mind, but I really wanted the Fruit Roll-Up. I felt so cool to have a wrapper that I kept crinkling it to get attention, as if to say, "Look, me too!" I ended up saving the wrapper and pulling it out on other days, pretending I had just finished my Fruit Roll - Up like everyone else so I could fit in better. Eventually I taped it in my notebook.

We also only received toys at Christmas or for our birthdays. My parents were not the type to buy us a toy when we were at a toy store, or out and about at any store. As a child, this is an amazingly difficult pill to swallow. A child psychologist has since informed me that kids view play as their job. Hardworking kids want new toys so they can expand the duties of their job. When I was in sixth grade, Nanopets and Tamagotchis became all the rage. I desperately wanted one, but my parents said they were junk and a waste of money. After realizing my pestering was not getting me anywhere, I took it in my own hands to make my own. I colored one of those small white cardboard boxes that jewelry comes in, and drew buttons and a fake screen with glitter pens. I would put it in my pocket and bring it to school. I told my friends I had one, and after showing the first girl my "new Tamagotchi," she laughed at me. So I kept it concealed in my pocket and said "it was sleeping." When I would take a bathroom break at school, I'd hide in the stall playing with my Tamagotchi, pretending to feed it and exercise it, like the real ones.

I was a child that did lots of activities and was fascinated by lots of things. I played numerous sports, was a Girl Scout from age four through the end of high school, participated on an Odyssey of the Mind team for several years, took piano, flute, and oboe lessons, played in a chamber music group, and did my own home research projects on various science topics such as crystals, constellations, and layers of the earth's crust. I took Japanese lessons with my sisters from age six to eleven, I enjoyed putting together as many jigsaw puzzles in an hour or two as I could assemble, and I loved board games. I was always laughing, making jokes, or asking Mom if I could help her in the kitchen. I loved cooking and wanted to be like my mom. If I was well behaved, she'd take me with her to the Farmer's Market in town on Saturday mornings and buy me a honey stick or a piece of maple candy – rare treats that I loved.

Our family was very close-knit. We spent the majority of our free time together. Our hobbies were a bit on the odd side – the main family activity was contra dancing. It's hard to call this just a hobby, because we were die-hard participants. I started going to contra dances when I could barely walk, and began learning the moves when I was three. My parents would take us to the local dances in New Hampshire, where we were living at the time, and we would dance until we were tired. Then they would roll out our sleeping bags in the corner of the dance hall and go to sleep until our parents were done dancing for the night. They would carry us in our bags out to the car.

When we were older, we went to a dance in Greenfield, MA, every Friday night and occasionally went to a local dance on Saturday nights as well. Several times per year, we would go on "Contra Dance Vacations." These were weekend or week-long folk dancing extravaganzas. I grew up around folk music. All of the contra dancers knew us, and I learned many by name. Wayne would always pull a magic trick out of his pocket to entertain me, and Ralph came armed with riddles.

4

We enjoyed many outdoor activities such as camping, hiking, backpacking, cross-country skiing, biking, and badminton. Weekend days, after chores were done, we played board games, swam in the pool during the summer, helped my mom with the gardening, or did all of the various errands together, all five of us in the car. We did spend time with friends, but that was a significantly smaller amount of time than family time. The vast majority of everything we did, including Girl Scouts, all five of us did together. My sisters were my best friends.

Sometimes people have asked me if my mom played in a role in the development of my anorexia. My mom was always the thinnest woman I knew. In fact, the irony is that during the peak of my anorexia, when I was about half the weight I should have been for my height, some of my peers asked me if my mom had an eating disorder because hers seemed more apparent than mine. My mom has never admitted to having an eating disorder, although spending any amount of time with her clearly indicates that she has disordered eating and a skewed body image.

My true belief is that almost everything plays a role, and it is how these factors interact that increases or decreases the chances of developing a severe eating disorder. Part of it was certainly my personality. I am a driven, Type A person, the type that research studies tend to show have a higher propensity for disordered eating, particularly anorexia nervosa. At the same time, I felt largely inadequate. I constantly compared myself to my sisters because I spent nearly all of my time with them. My sisters were older than me, and in childhood development, each year brings a lot of change – increased knowledge, maturity, improvement in fine motor skills, and the like. Beginning when I was five, I started comparing myself to them, not understanding that I deserved a handicap because I was younger.

I started piano when I was four, a year after they had already been playing. I struggled to master rhythm, even though I learned to read music quickly. Ashleigh and Emily were great, and, because they were both at a similar advanced level, they played duets together. I played by myself and cried during my lessons a few times when I was told my rhythm was terrible. Holly, our teacher, was not gentle. One time, she made me stomp out the rhythm of a song in our front yard, my eyes blurry with tears. She also gave us "ear training" homework: a recording of her playing various chords. Our job was to write the notes or chords she was playing. I was terrible at this, and always scored lower than Ashleigh and Emily. I used to get butterflies in my stomach every Wednesday on the bus home from school, panicking about my impending lesson: 30 minutes of torture.

We took private Japanese lessons together with a teacher that would come to our house. I almost always scored lower in quizzes, struggled at the competitive games to answer as rapidly, and was not as quick at mastering the language. Our teacher did not help bring light to the fact that I was simply younger. She often compared us out loud and reprimanded me for getting something incorrect that Ashleigh and Emily knew. I had behavioral problems that my parents had never dealt with in my older sisters. My teachers, on multiple occasions, told my parents that I was out of control. Neither Emily nor Ashleigh had ADHD, and both were always praised for being well-behaved role models in class. I was the kid whose parents got notes and calls about the ways I interrupted, distracted, or otherwise derailed a lesson in school. I felt like I disappointed them.

2.
The Ball Pit

IT IS DIFFICULT TO pinpoint what exactly changed me. One day, I was a child who looked in the mirror and saw a superhero; the next, I saw someone worthless and inadequate. This was probably largely due to feeling like I was disappointing my parents, that I could not control my behavior even though I genuinely wanted to, and my perception that I was not living up to the expectations of others.

Many experts think anorexia develops somewhat unconsciously. Perhaps, because I was so young, it was different for me, but it was definitely a conscious decision. The irony is, even though running would become the main motivation behind my prolonged restriction of food, when I began having problems with eating, I wasn't even a runner yet. On top of that, I was already the smallest in my elementary school class, and I certainly did not need to lose any weight. I had always been a slow grower and below the 5th percentile for height and weight for my age, even as a toddler. However, none of this ended up convincing me that I did not need to lose weight.

There were a few key elements that I think contributed to the development of my eating disorder. The first occurred around early December when I was in the fifth grade – 10 years old. I didn't know very much at all about puberty, and frankly, everything I did know scared me to death. I liked being a kid, and the only experience I had with "teenagers" was through my oldest sister, Ashleigh. One particularly vivid memory occurred when we were en route to Cape Cod to visit my grandparents. We were at a music recital of some sort and Ashleigh and my mom spent forever in the bathroom (or what seemed like forever). As I impatiently continued to evaluate the holdup, I heard words that stuck with me. *Period. Blood. Napkin to stop bleeding.* I didn't know what a period was, but I was worried that Ashleigh was dying. I knew it had something to do with crying, blood, and bathrooms. That night when we got to Cape Cod, we all assumed our usual sleeping positions - the kids in the basement, my parents upstairs. I lay awake on my grandma's red couch. As my sisters slept peacefully, I watched the numbers flip on the clock, its hum my only company. *Is Ashleigh going to die from "the period?"* Somehow, I temporarily got over it, and heard nothing about periods until fifth grade. I still wasn't sure what my sister "had" and if she was okay.

In fifth grade we had health units through a program called *The Great Body Shop*. One week, the topic of puberty surfaced. I can't recall anything about the lesson except learning more about the infamous period - and the overwhelming feeling of fear that filled me. It sounded awful. The key thing that I learned through the lesson was that at a certain body fat percentage, boys and girls would begin going through puberty. It became my mission to stay a kid for as long as I could by keeping low body fat. I didn't exactly know what this meant, or how to do it, yet I was an extremely bright child. I knew if I ate less, I'd be less fat, and that was really all the information that I needed.

The second major thing that happened during this time was a family scandal of sorts. To this day, it's not something I know much about, but the basic information that is important to know is that my parents were called in to an emergency meeting at the middle school where Ashleigh was an eighth grader. My sister was implicated in cocaine use by several of her peers, and this was brought to the attention of my parents. The only things I knew about drugs were from the D.A.R.E (Drug Abuse Resistance Education) Program, and I was pretty sure my sister would never be one of those movie characters with needles coming out of her arms. My mom didn't say anything when she picked me up from school that day. In fact, I believe we canceled the Girl Scouts' meeting. I overheard my mother, father, and Ashleigh talking that afternoon, but I really had no idea what was going on.

That evening, I went to a joint birthday party for three of my friends at Kidsports – a local recreation facility. Like all small towns, the ladies of Amherst loved to gossip. As I was playing on scooters with my friends at the party, I heard a group of several of the moms talking about the drug scandal that day, because they had older daughters my sister's age who were involved in the accusations of my sister. I scooted over within earshot to listen to the story. They were all saying my sister was a drug addict and then one of the mothers mentioned my name – "The little girl wearing yellow, Amber, yeah, she's her sister." I felt ashamed and confused. I left my little red scooter and tiptoed to the ball pit. I buried myself under a pile of plastic balls while the rest of the kids ran to the table for pizza and cake. I figured as long as I was hidden, I was safe and so was my sister. I was relieved to miss the gathering of people eating pizza and cake. I didn't want other kids pointing or staring at me. I felt that by hiding away, I had successfully controlled the situation.

The party was a sleepover, and everyone dragged their sleeping bags all over the structure at Kidsports. I stayed put in the ball pit. I wanted people to forget about me, and luckily none of the parents ever came looking. Even as my stomach rumbled and I eventually became cold under the plastic balls, I felt a sense of safety. I felt like I was protecting my family. Moreover, I felt rewarded that I had not eaten the pizza and cake. *It's what my family would want*, I thought.

The night stretched on minute by minute. *Don't worry, I won't let anyone say bad things about you, Ash.* When morning finally came and kids started to leave, I stealthily climbed out of the ball pit and waited for my parents to get me. It was a quiet ride home. I was tired from my sleepless night, and my parents looked much more exhausted. I knew that home must have been tense.

To this day, I believe Ashleigh was not using or involved with any drugs, but because that was the worry, my parents, rightfully so, became extremely obsessed that this may be the case. I felt like I was becoming the background – a shadow without a face. My needs became less important; my behavior went unnoticed.

The trouble was, I always had some insecurities, but at the time I didn't know where they came from. As the youngest of three girls, I always felt somehow like I was a disappointment. My two older sisters are honestly angels. I had nothing but the best role models. They were smart, helpful, cheerful, well-behaved, organized, and beautiful. I, although smart, was the only one with behavioral problems – and pretty severe ADHD from a young age. My father couldn't stand my hyperactivity or wild energy. When I crossed the line in his opinion (which, I think, was set much too low for a five-, six-, or seven-year old), or my silliness got the better of him, he took out his frustration on me physically. I never once saw him scold either of my sisters the way he scolded me when I was in trouble. This may be due to the fact that they did not get on his nerves as much – or perhaps being the youngest, I was just the straw that broke the camel's back. As a result, I became scared of him and felt like he didn't love me as much as he loved Ashleigh or Emily.

I was constantly reprimanded throughout elementary school, particularly when I was younger, for being out of control, being a distraction to others, not being in control of my body or my laughter. I could not sit still. In first grade, we had a classroom store. Kids would bring in old toys to resell in the store, and we would earn paper coins at the end of each day based on good behavior – things like being quiet during circle time, helping hand out papers, or standing quietly in line. Being so hyper lent itself to earning very few coins every day.

My best friend in first grade was a Japanese exchange student, Shotaro. He knew not a lick of English and was the sweetest, most helpful little boy. Our "conversations" were either silent, simultaneous play, or consisted of hand gestures, nods, and smiles. Shotaro racked up so many coins that sometimes, if he felt very bad for me, he'd sneak me one in the parking lot where I would wait before my mom would pick me up. On Wednesdays, we had the chance to "shop" at the classroom store with our coins. I never had enough money. There was a pink periscope I had my eye on, but when it was my turn to shop and I only had fifteen cents

($1.35 less than I needed), Corey Winkler snatched it up. He also bought the Cabbage Patch Kid – my second choice.

Meanwhile, I felt like I was disappearing from my parents' attention after the incident with Ashleigh the night of the Kidsports party. No one at home wanted to play with me; it felt like my stories didn't matter. I quietly tried to fly under the radar in my bedroom. This brings me to the last piece of the puzzle.

Some weeks later, we took a family trip to Boston, where we often enjoyed going. After a day at the Museum of Science and walking around Cambridge, we went to eat at a food court. Normally, this would be a very "un-Sayer" activity, but for some reason, we ended up here for dinner. I remember it being one of the first times I was ever in a food court. The multitude of colors, lights, booths, food choices, and smells immediately overwhelmed me. I think my parents were also bewildered, and they split us up to divide and conquer the challenge of purchasing dinner. Dad took my sisters; Mom took me.

My mom was a health nut. She raised us vegetarian, she was a runner herself –embarking on 3-4 mile runs every morning at 5:30 a.m. while I still lay in bed – and we always ate health food. On this particular day, I desperately wanted to win the approval of my mom. It had been several weeks since the incident with my sister, and with each passing week, I felt like I was slipping further from her halo of attention. This issue came on top of the usual fear that I had never seemed to be at all like my mom, and I worried that was the reason why she was frequently disappointed in me. As we walked anxiously around the food court, Mom asked me what I wanted to eat, offering to get me anything I wanted. After a minute of deliberation, I said, "I want what you are having." Mom said she was going to have just a salad, and I probably wanted something else. Deep down I wanted the soft-serve ice cream sundae with hot fudge. I salivated as I imagined digging my big plastic spoon into a cup teeming with toppings. Snapping back to reality, I replied, "That's okay. I want a salad like you!"

As our family squished together into the booth that night eating our finds, I felt happy to look over and see Mom and I eating the same thing. For the first time in years, I felt like "Mommy's girl." That night when we were leaving the food court, my mom took my hand and said, "I'm so proud of you for choosing a healthy salad when you could have had any of the food there." I felt like I had won her approval, and I had just discovered a secret to her heart. (Now that I am a mature adult, I understand that there was no secret to her heart – I already had it. But kids can misinterpret things.)

So I took these pieces of information – that I needed to have as little body fat as I could to remain a kid, and I should eat like Mom for her to love me more and for me to be less of a disappointment – to synthesize an action plan: I would begin to diet. I grew up in a fat-phobic family, because that was the era. Susan Powter championed the slogan "fat makes you fat." When my sisters and I were growing up, my family definitely embraced Powter's message, so that's what I "knew" about dieting. I quickly learned how to read nutrition labels, how many calories were in certain foods, and how to make lower fat choices – things many American adults still don't know. (As an aside, now that it's 2013, we know that Susan Powter was wrong – fat does *not* make you fat, in and of itself.) I didn't really understand the concept of counting calories, but it was only grams of fat I thought I needed to be concerned with. I remember trying to count all the grams of fat consumed each day on my fingers in the shower and wanting less than fifteen. Fifteen was good for Sundays – pancake and homemade pizza day. Every other day, it needed to be less than that.

I had no trouble sticking with this plan because we lived in a very "low-fat" house. Basically all of our choices were low-fat, and I would opt for the lowest fat option. I remember in sixth grade, since I packed my own lunches and snacks for school, I started to change what I brought. There had been times I would bring a Lender's bagel with cream cheese (low-fat of course), as well as various other snacks. I switched to jelly on the bagel instead of cream cheese, since it had no fat. Additionally, I noticed that one of the packages of Lender's cinnamon raisin bagels had zero grams of fat, while another package with just a slightly darker label had one gram of fat. It was my mission to be the "bagel-fetcher" during grocery shopping excursions so I could make sure the freezer was stocked with the fat-free variety.

Another important change I made was to cut out "junk food" that contained fat, which was most junk food. As a child, I always had a prominent sweet tooth. I loved ice cream, cupcakes, cookies, doughnuts, you name it. We rarely ate any of the pastry-type items, but we had ice cream (again low-fat) nearly every night before bed. Once my diet began, I stopped eating corn chips, Girl Scout cookies, and homemade cookies – basically all of the few non-health foods we ate. With the exception of a small mug of frozen yogurt most nights after dinner, this remained a restriction throughout the anorexia.

3.

"Pound for Pound, You're the Strongest of the Sayers"

BOTH OF MY PARENTS ran recreationally. Their daily endeavor was never a big part of my relationship with them, and something I knew very little about because it took place before I woke up, and they never participated in races in my childhood. When I was in sixth grade, Ashleigh was a freshman in high school and joined the cross-country team.

I was a fairly athletic child. Born into an active family, I had to keep up, even though I was the youngest. My mom was an aerobics instructor when I was still in diapers, and I would take swimming lessons while she taught class. When I got a little older, I'd wear the bathing suit to her class instead of the pool and jump around with the older women. I learned to take my pulse when I was four. I thought it was so cool that all the people were looking to Mom to tell them how to move. Plus, the music was sassy and I liked the steps.

As a family, we did long, hilly bike treks and hikes up to twelve miles long with 30-pound packs. This was their idea of fun. I complained. Because I was so small for my age, even as a young child, the trips were exhausting. My dad often hung back with me as I struggled to pedal up the steep hills of the Vermont countryside. "Pound for pound, you're the strongest of the Sayers," he'd tell me.

I hung in there during all of the physical excursions, and I was strong and tough because of them. My endurance was great. I started formal soccer and basketball on the community recreational leagues in fourth grade, and I could outrun all the girls. Coaches called me the Energizer Bunny. In fact, one of our basketball coaches drafted a play where I literally ran around in crazy patterns, trying to tire out my defender. With little legs, I wasn't especially fast, but I could keep going.

In the spring at my elementary school, starting in fourth or fifth grade, we did the mile run on the cinder track as part of the physical education curriculum. I don't remember running well those first two years - probably because I got distracted with the task and made a dandelion crown halfway through - but in sixth grade, with a pair of jeans and Timberland hiking boots, I ran 8:08. I beat most of the boys, except two who lived in Amherst woods and were known as "the athletes." My physical education teacher, who also happened to be one of my neighbors, told me I should run cross-country in middle school - just a few months away. I felt proud, like there was a job for me that I should fulfill. *Cross-country? Just like Ashleigh, and she doesn't even know that Ashleigh runs!*

Another thing about my childhood personality was that I believed in "signs." It wasn't anything I ever verbalized, and in fact, I didn't call them "signs" in my head, but I believed things I saw and connected dots on my own to create what I considered the full picture. For instance, when we were kids, my sisters and I would have a sleepover every Christmas Eve. We would crowd in Emily's room - Ashleigh and Emily in the bunk beds, and me on the floor in my sleeping bag. My dad would read us *The Polar Express* and *The Night Before Christmas*. After he would leave, my sisters and I would talk about all the gifts we hoped we would be getting come morning and discuss evidence we had amassed as to why we thought someone might be getting a specific gift. "Well when I was with Mom at CVS, I SAW her buy the Tic-Tacs you like!"

When I was six-years old, wise, honest Ashleigh told me that Santa Claus was not real. I was in shock, as I'm sure all kids are at that age. I didn't believe her and I made it my mission to try to prove that he was real. Earlier that December I had drafted a list of gifts I wanted for Christmas, and after Ashleigh laughed and pointed out the fact that nothing was spelled correctly, I tearfully threw my list away. I never showed the wish list to my parents, and when they asked what I wanted, I'm sure I shrugged and said "arts and crafts." However, one of the things I listed – and to this day I have no idea why – was a fish. Well, Christmas morning, I got a fish from Santa. *How would Mom and Dad have known?*

The following year, there was a bigger log to throw on the fire. "Santa" brought Emily a rabbit. Yet, that morning on our way home from church I saw a rabbit in a big cage in the back of Dad's car. *He must have bought her a rabbit too, but when he saw that Santa brought her one overnight, Dad figured he needed to return the one he chose.* I still don't know if there were two rabbits, a miscommunication between parents, or a quickly-moved cage. Needless to say, these were strong "signs" to me that Santa existed, and I was pretty confident he did until a year or so later, when I'm sure clearer "signs" proved he didn't.

Back to the gym teacher. Her suggestion that I should run cross-country, without even knowing that was an activity my family members did, was a "sign" to me that I was destined to run. It was on that afternoon, panting breathlessly in the field after running the mile, that I decided I should be a runner.

Throughout middle school, I continued to play soccer and basketball on the recreational teams. I had dropped softball after seventh grade because I was utterly terrible. But the older I got, the more substantial my injuries became. Game day was slaughter day. During basketball games, I ran fearlessly into girls almost twice my weight, and would get tripped up and then go flying head-first into the gym floor like a catapult, the other girl standing strong like a wall in my tracks. I got bloody noses, scraped knees, bruises that made me look like a plum, and yet I kept on playing. I was aggressive. Finally my parents decided it was too painful to watch the dozens of tumbles, and they pulled me from contact sports. Cross-country it would be.

The first day of cross-country in seventh grade, I re-met the girl who would become my best friend through my senior year of high school – Samantha Winters.* I say re-met, because we had seen each other about once a year since I was five-years old at a

---

* Name changed

mutual friend's birthday party. But because Samantha lived in Shutesbury, we had nothing to do with each other except that one day a year at Brooke's party. I actually always felt a little threatened by Samantha as a young child. Seeing myself as Brooke's best friend, I wondered, *who's this other girl that always comes here?*

Samantha and I saw each other at the benches in front of the school where interested seventh graders were told to meet. Sheepishly, we approached one another after seeing that neither one of us had brought a friend to the first practice. It was friendship at first sight.

Janda, our coach, was a tall, lean, shaven-legged super-athlete. He had calves bigger than any I had ever seen in real life, and an Adam's apple that literally looked like an apple glued onto his neck. I was scared. "We are going to head down to the track and run," he said. And that's what we did. All he wanted to do was see how many laps we could do without stopping or giving up. When you were done running, you went to the water fountain to stretch. I ran around and around the track. I think I did seven laps (about 1.75 miles)– which, for a seventh-grade girl, was killer. I hung with a group of boys. After practice, Janda pulled me aside. "You're good. Have you run before?" I told him that I had trained some during the summer and that my family had runners in it. "Good." Practices were fun. I ran with him and a group of boys. We would stop and walk at times, but I quickly improved my endurance.

My first race was the Amherst Invitational Two-Mile Middle School race at Hampshire College. I had never run any sort of road race or track race in my life. I was nervous but excited. I knew I could run two miles without walking, because I had already done it in practice – but when the gun went off, everything changed. Running was hard! I got a buckling side stitch a quarter-mile into the race. Every breath was painful. I held my side and limped on. Atop a small hill under a tree, about a mile through the race, I saw my dad. "Can I stop?" I asked. "Keep going, Am," he urged, sounding somewhat miffed that I even asked. I didn't want to let him down. I kept going. I finished tenth in 15:21. I was the first seventh grader on my team to finish, and that made me proud. I was handed a green ribbon, and it was the first award I got that wasn't just for participating. The gold lettering sparkled in the bright September sun. *I won this!*

I continued to improve throughout the seventh grade cross-country season. I was doing increasingly better in races, loving every minute of it. The season was short, however, and when it was over, a few friends and I decided we would do the Junior Olympics. It was the first time I began to coach myself and decide how long, where, and how fast I would train. Sometimes, in my solitude, I would recite Dad's old mantra through my head: *pound for pound, you're the strongest of the Sayers. Make them proud.*

Every day after school, even as November brought her bitter air, I ran alone, with the goal of running well at Junior Olympics. I wasn't running much – maybe three miles – but I was developing remarkable toughness and an ability to force myself to train, even when it felt like I would rather go home and play. As I loped along the roads of Amherst, I would think about running in the Olympics someday or winning a really big race. I wondered what breaking through finish tape would feel like. I thought about the meaning of my dad's mantra. I figured that if I was smaller but still just as strong, I'd be even stronger "pound for pound."

My running improved significantly between seventh and eighth grade. In seventh grade, during cross-country, I was up near the front of most races, and in track, I ran 7:21 in the mile. In eighth grade, I started winning races, leading the pack, and ran a 5:45 mile in track. I attribute much of the improvement to my summer training between seventh and eighth grade and the continual, sequential elimination of foods from my diet, as well as the central focus that running began to take in my life. Running slowly began to supplant my other childhood interests.

4.
Junior Olympics in Eighth Grade

IN EIGHTH GRADE, I also competed in the Junior Olympics in both cross-country and track. In cross-country, I qualified for the National Championships in Spartanburg, South Carolina, after getting fourth place in the Association meet and sixteenth place in the Regional race. I can't recall that much about the experience, except the feeling during the regional race when I exited the woods at Van Cortland Park in the Bronx, and someone yelled to me, "Number seventeen!" I knew that the top twenty made it to the National Championships. *Just don't let three people pass you. Just don't let three people pass you.* In the final stretch I kept trucking along, passing one girl nearly twice my height.

My mom took the trip to Spartanburg with me, along with two of my friends, James and Ian, and their mothers. The details of the trip are mainly lost in my mind these days, but I remember that it was the first real trip my running afforded me, and the beginning of years of traveling with my mom to big races. I recall a rush of pride overwhelming me as I ascended the escalator in the Greenville-Spartanburg airport and saw the huge banner proclaiming, "Welcome Junior Olympics National Championship Participants!" I recall sitting with my mom at the Ramada's buffet breakfast and watching people belly flop in the hotel pool. I also distinctly remember I was one of the few runners on the line who still wore training shoes rather than racing spikes; I think my feet were still too small for spikes. Most importantly, the trip planted a seed in my mind that my running had the powerful potential of truly enriching my life.

5.
"Let me wear my Tevas"

ONE OF THE CHALLENGES of my early days of running was finding appropriate shoes. Now, in full disclosure, I admit that when I started running, every day I ran in a full nylon green track suit that I got at the consignment store in town. It was the end of sixth grade in late June. It was hot. More interestingly, I wore Teva sandals for a few weeks while I trained, because I wanted to "feel like an Olympian." Somehow, running in sandals made me envision that I was some sort of Ancient Greek Olympic hero. Yeah, I was a weird kid.

After a few stubbed toes and twisted ankles, I quickly got over the Teva phase. My mom took me to the specialty running store, The Runner's Shop, in the nearby town of Northampton. I fell in love with the place the moment the bell jingled as the door closed behind me. My eyes scanned the walls of shoes, racks of running clothing, and posters adorning the walls of elite runners, who I called in my mind "the champs." The problem was, back when I was just turning twelve, kid-specific running equipment was not as readily available as it is today. The store carried suitable items for the average-sized twelve-year-old, but not one the size of a six-year-old. The owner was kind enough to special-order a pair of Nike Triax 2 sneakers in youth size 1.5. I still remember the model number. The shoes were masculine-looking – white, black, and green – but they were my first running shoes and I loved them.

Just days before seventh grade started, my mom took me to Kmart to get me my first sports bra. It was a matching sports bra and underwear set, and it eventually became the same "lucky" sports bra and underwear I raced in through my junior year of high school (of course, washed a zillion times – unlike some runners!). I still had a little kid's body and certainly didn't need a sports bra. However, Amherst athletic teams wore white shirts, and girls shouldn't wear white shirts without a bra during sports. Thankfully, my mom was aware of this fashion "rule" and suggested I get one. This was a relief, because it meant that I didn't need to tell her that Jen Tyson had pulled my shirt down past my chest during band practice and yelled, "You still don't wear a bra?!!"

For the first six months of my life, I wore a hip brace because I was born with severely misaligned hips. While I slept, my infant body was fastened into a contraption consisting of Velcro straps and connecting pieces in an attempt to correct the imbalance. It was clear as soon as I could stand that I had incredibly flat feet that pronated severely. I was in orthotics by the time I could walk. Emily and I both had orange, hard plastic orthotics that we were fitted for annually. One time, we were jumping rope in the driveway, and her orthotics cracked all the way through as she landed. They were not comfortable, and because they were so thick and inflexible, we could only buy certain sneakers – always "high tops" and usually ugly, wide hiking boot-like shoes. I even wore them playing basketball. We were only free from wearing the orthotics on special occasions when we wore "girly shoes" – little patent leather flats, jelly shoes, or slippers.

When I started running, I did not run in my orthotics. The specialists at The Runner's Shop noted that I actually ran with more natural biomechanics than when I walked. My feet landed without rolling in as I floated down the road. I felt fast in my sneakers without the big orthotics, and in my mind, it was another "sign" that I was a natural-born runner. Sometimes the ideas in your mind dictate your behaviors and outcomes. Because I felt like a natural runner, I trained as if I was supposed to be the best, and because I trained harder than virtually all of the other eleven-year-old girls in my area, I became better than my peers.

I had a vision of what being an "elite" runner would be like and feel like. I imagined people asking me for advice about their training, excited to meet me and share their story, hoping to be just like me. I pictured myself competing in races, traveling around the country, or even the world, representing an athletic company such as Nike. Races would take me to places I could not even imagine. I would get the opportunity to learn about different cultures through the running community that would welcome me on my visit. I envisioned that the small children in these foreign countries, upon recognizing me from the television, would come running up, falling into stride beside me, joyously giggling as they joined me on a jaunt through their village.

As an elite runner, I would teach seminars on nutrition, programming, and race strategy. Sporting goods companies would send me free sneakers and running clothing, which, as a young runner, was a very exciting prospect. Schools around the nation would invite me to come and speak to student athletes about overcoming adversities, the benefits of athletics, and their importance to education.

When I experienced pain, I would have a team of trainers and physicians able to quickly diagnose me and send me on my way. I would train with a group of other professional runners – a small, tight-knit community of like-minded women, chasing the same dreams side by side. I could work out at altitude, take a recovery day in the pool, or cruise along a mountain pass on a long run.

The most exciting promise of becoming an elite runner was that my family would be proud of me and I would bind us all together, representing "the Sayers" in a successful light for life.

6.
WayCoolRunning Forum

STARTING IN SEVENTH GRADE, I joined an online forum for teenage runners called WayCoolRunning – a sister site of coolrunning.com. I mostly read posts from other runners, eventually adding my own ideas about training, answered questions, and shared my race experiences. I quickly made two "online friends": Stephen and Kevin, from a team in Connecticut. They became instant fans and very eager to chat online with me about my training, as they were very impressed with my caliber. We started chatting on AIM – an online instant chat application – where we supported one another's running careers and I offered answers to their questions. Because they solicited my advice, I felt needed and appreciated, and as an incredibly shy girl, I felt relieved to be able to help people from behind the safety of my computer screen rather than face-to-face.

We talked over the next few years. However, with Stephen, conversations started to veer from running to personal life. Eventually, my naive mind understood he had a crush on me. He sent me a valentine, wrote several love poems, and asked if he could drive up and see me. I wasn't interested in a romantic relationship despite the fact he told me he looked like "a young Tom Hanks." I later found out he had bent the truth on his age, lobbing three years off, and he was significantly older than me. I disabled my account and feared he'd track me down and surprise me at a race.

7.
How to Earn a Star Sticker

ONE AFTERNOON IN THE beginning of eighth grade, I was
scrutinized by the pediatrician at a standard "weigh-in"
appointment. My weight was no longer flat-lined – it had begun
dropping fairy consistently. Standing with an open-back gown in a
freezing cold exam room, my pediatrician showed my mom how all
along my spine, scapulae, and where my hip bones protruded in
the back, my skin appeared bruised. Because the fat under my skin
(subcutaneous fat) was virtually non-existent, my bones were not
padded by anything except a thin layer of skin. When I lay on my
back, the bones in the posterior of my body gnawed through my
skin, leaving it bruised and discolored. It was painful to the touch,
but I hadn't noticed it until the pediatrician and my mom poked
and prodded the bony protrusions in places I couldn't see. When I
got home that afternoon, I looked closely in the mirror. *It's like a
cartoon drawing of a skeleton lightly tattooed on my back.*

Around the same time, I started doing crunches compulsively.
I would eventually try to get in 1,000 per day, every day – 500 in
the morning and 500 at some other point. It began with just the
morning 500, but then I doubled it when that seemed to be paying
off for me. The crunches were something I did privately – a covert
activity I snuck into my regimen that I thought would provide me
with an extra edge. My parents kept fairly close tabs on my physical
activity level, since they were trying to limit caloric expenditure
and promote weight gain. My rug was too hard and I didn't have a
yoga mat, so I discovered the bathroom floor rug was the most
comfortable and seamless way to accomplish my crunches. After
all, everyone has to go to the bathroom, so I figured that no one
would suspect I was exercising in there. It would take me a little

more than six minutes to complete 500 (sounds effective, right?). These highly repetitive motions probably contributed to the bruising along my back.

Our house had two full bathrooms upstairs and one half bathroom downstairs. "The girls" shared one of the full bathrooms, and the other was used exclusively by my parents. Since I used "the girls'" for my crunches, my sisters would often try to get in there, yelling that I was in there for "hours." Seven minutes is a long time in the world of a teenage girl waiting to get ready for school. But I would just say to them that I was almost done while I hurried through the remaining few hundred crunches.

If I completed my 1,000 crunches in a day, I would give myself a little star sticker – the kind my parents had given me years before when I made it through a night without sucking my thumb. I would take the star from my stash in my sticker book and carefully paste it into a small journal kept in my desk. The journal was actually a stack of papers that I stapled together into a booklet. I figured that it looked less interesting this way, so my sisters or my parents wouldn't snoop and read it. My oldest sister, Ashleigh, had the annoying habit of rummaging through my desk drawers, finding my real journal, and reading it aloud, much to my embarrassment. It was as if she was doing this to make fun of me, not to get to know me better. Her motives were one of an older sister picking on a younger, trivializing my experiences, emotions, and ideas. But the stapled papers looked like a junky art project and remained un-pillaged. Occasionally, before a cross-country or track meet that I was particularly nervous about, I would flip through the pages of my homemade journal and see all the stars. *I've done a lot of hard work. I am ready.*

8.
Advent of Sneaking

WHEN I WAS IN eighth grade, my sisters and I got Advent calendars from Atkins Country Market, a grocery store in our town. We were raised Catholic and attended church every Sunday morning. (During my first confession in the fourth grade, I confessed to being "sometimes mean to my sisters and loving desserts too much.") We all went to CCD (Sunday school) through the end of high school. Therefore, we celebrated Christmas in a more religious rather than secular fashion. For Advent, we had an Advent wreath on our kitchen table, and we would light the candles and say prayers for the season of Advent preceding Christmas. Candy Advent calendars were a thing for "regular" kids. However, this particular year we got them because they were on clearance at Atkins for $3.00. Each day counting down toward Christmas had a corresponding door scattered along a bright cartoon drawing of a pagan Christmas scene – Santa with a bag of toys, a Christmas tree covered with ornaments, or a rooftop scene with Santa's reindeer and a sack of toys. Behind each door was a small piece of milk chocolate in a Christmas-themed shape.

As a young girl, I always wanted an Advent calendar. Kids don't have the same understanding of how time passes, and Christmas always seemed to take eons to finally arrive. I used to make paper-link chains counting down the days and rip off a link every day, but I yearned for the commercial calendar with the doors concealing chocolates. These seemed like a magical blend of surprise and treat.

When I finally got one, I was choco-phobic. I did not want the stuff to pass my lips and virtually never let it. I scanned the back of the calendar. Serving size: 12 pieces. Servings per container: about

2. Calories per serving: 190. And there it was, glaring back at me: Total Fat: 11 grams. That meant each little piece had almost one full gram of fat. *Kill me. I can't eat that!* The new "game" became how to dispose of the chocolates while making it look like I was eating them. Sometimes I pretended I had just put the candy in my mouth, sucking on a creamy chocolate morsel while I secretly held it in my lightly clasped fist or slipped it into my pocket or book bag to discard later. Other times I popped it out on the kitchen counter while running the sink to get a cold glass of water. I would covertly drop it down the garbage disposal and run it, saying it looked like the water was not draining. I managed to not eat a single one of the chocolates. Advent became 25 days of avoiding a treat.

That behavior shames me now. Being sneaky and dishonest is exactly what my Christian morals taught me not to do. In my heart I knew better and knew that it wasn't like me to be deceptive, but in my anorexic mind, it was as if I was on autopilot, going mindlessly through the motions of denying myself the treat at whatever cost.

9.
Winter Warriors

IN EIGHTH GRADE, ONCE cross-country season and the Junior Olympic Championships were over, I started running in the early morning. My parents had always run at 5:30 am and for some reason, they convinced my sisters and I that this was going to be the best time for us to run until spring, because it would be dark in the evening anyway. To this day, I'm not sure why we did this, because although I had some afterschool activities, most afternoons I recall being at home with Ashleigh, bored and struggling to be productive with homework, craving the mental break from academia that running usually provided between school and homework time in the evening.

Emily would run with my mom, Dad usually decided everyone was too fast for him and "did his own short thing," and I would run with Ashleigh, the same route as Emily and Mom, just at a faster pace. Emily had recently started running and was still working on building her endurance. Ashleigh and I, the cross-country runners, would lead the chase. I would roll out of bed fifteen minutes after 5:00 am and head to the bathroom to bang out my 500 crunches. Then I would layer up, sometimes even wearing a full facemask, to greet the freezing New England winter morning.

In the darkness, we carried headlamps – one for each pair of us, since we didn't have one for everyone. The halos of light under the street lamps were sometimes the only parts we could see. We told each other about the patches of black ice, or where the tire tracks were on mornings that there was snow. Usually Ashleigh and I didn't talk much. Our neck warmers were wet with perspiration that, upon hitting the sub-ten degree air, would freeze, forming ice around our noses and mouths. Ashleigh wore glasses that would completely fog up as the heat from her body got trapped under the lenses and the cold air blanketed the front. When it was time to turn onto a new street, I was the guide. "This way, Ash," I'd say, startled by the sound of my own voice in the silent darkness.

We usually did one of three routes. Two were nearly identical, with the addition of an extra add-on road on one of them. The other went the opposite way from our house. I liked the two longer runs, each about three miles. One of them was especially fun because we would run by the house of a guy Ashleigh had a crush on. "Let's go fast past Ryan's and then we'll slow down again." I'd laugh and we'd run fast, as if he would be looking out his window at quarter to six. Ashleigh and I were not the same pace. I had the ability to run substantially faster than her, but we were good partners. I enjoyed my time with her, even if it was cold and mostly silent. We were warriors of the quiet snow-crusted roads, tackling the icy darkness. While we were running, we were at peace. We helped one another through the cold, and I was her eyes, helping her see.

Once back in the house, we'd take off our wet layers and fall into our usual routine relationship, fighting over who would shower first, what time we were leaving for school, or to stop laughing so loud. The run was our moment of harmony, and I loved that. Being four years younger than Ashleigh, I longed to have more involvement in her life, but as she grew up in high school, I became "too immature," "too hyper," or "wouldn't understand her."

The morning runs brought our relationship back together, eventually trickling into other parts of our lives. She would hang out with me at home after school, let me in her room to listen to music with her, or ask me if I needed help with homework. When spring rolled around, it would be light out by the time we rounded our street, Alpine Drive, on the return home, as if we'd run out of the darkness. It was still cold, but usually we would no longer need our neck warmers and thick mittens. Always someone who hated the cold, I was glad spring was coming, but I was also surprisingly sad that the winter was over and I would be starting outdoor track, leaving the morning runs with Ashleigh just a memory as I stayed in bed the extra half hour.

It was the last time we ran together regularly. There were rare instances, once I was in high school, that we would go on a run together, but that one winter during eighth grade will always be a special memory of my excursions with Ashleigh while most of Amherst slept.

10.
Eighth Grade: Banned from Running

SHORTLY AFTER THE OUTDOOR track season began, my parents pulled me from the team, and prohibited me for running because I was too thin. I was devastated. The birds were chirping, the grass was a mushy, muddy spring mess inviting me to train, and the air smelled like melting snow and flowering trees, but I wasn't allowed to run under any circumstance until I had gained five pounds.

My parents were very strict about the ban, and started coming home right after work or ensuring one of my sisters was home with me after school, so that I couldn't sneak in a run. The attitude wasn't a supportive "just gain five pounds and you're good to go!" but rather a constant feeling of punishment, as if I had committed a severe crime. I was essentially on lockdown. I was driven to school, and then expected on the bus home with one of my sisters from the high school. I was not to get any exercise.

After a few days of complying with my new restriction, I decided I would run anyway. The only available time that I discovered to be an option was right before school, after I was dropped off. My father was always anxious to get us to school early so he could get to work promptly. I was usually dropped off at the middle school by 7:10 or 7:15 a.m., and I was fortunate that both of my sisters were whisked to the high school. School didn't start until 7:50 and in fact, students were not usually allowed beyond the lobby until 7:20.

After Dad pulled away, I would walk with my backpack up behind the school, where part of the cross-country course passed along the ridge. I would hide my backpack in a bush and run in my school clothes – twill pants and a sweater. I ran back and forth on the ridge, not wanting to venture off the school property where anyone might see me, and needing to stay close to my backpack. I could usually get in 20 to 25 minutes. After retrieving my backpack, I would race into school. As I settled into my assigned desk in homeroom, little beads of sweat dripped down the perimeter of my face. One time my homeroom teacher asked if I was feeling okay. "Just fine," I replied, happy that I had managed to eke out a run and ready to face the school day.

11.
30 Laps

THE SUMMER AFTER EIGHTH grade, I attended Kinhaven Music Camp – a two-week music camp in Vermont where I played oboe in various groups, had private lessons, and was immersed in music. The camp took place at the end of August, just before the start of my first high school cross-country season, and I desperately wanted to be in good shape. Over that summer, I had trained harder than I ever had previously and was happy with my fitness. In eighth grade, cross-country races were a maximum of two miles, and most were between 1.5 and 1.8 miles (three kilometers). High school cross-country runners in Massachusetts typically raced five kilometers (3.1 miles), so there was a marked increase, and I wanted to ensure my endurance was sufficient.

Because I was such a young camper at Kinhaven, the counselors would not let me off the campus. Although the campus was gorgeous, it was only about one acre, and I was used to running three, four, or even five miles. I did not let this deter me. In the early mornings before we had to wake up for breakfast, I would put on my running shoes and jog down to a small field, where I would do laps. It took me just under a minute to do one lap. I would do thirty laps or so (I would lose count, but I relied on my watch and quite frankly, I would hit the same pace around that field like clockwork). The field was lumpy and mossy. I opted not to use the groomed sports field because it was too flat and tiny, only taking about forty seconds to get around. In the lumpy, secluded field, I could pass the time by enjoying the rolling patches, the uncharted path around the field that I would run. I felt like an explorer. Sure it was boring, but it was less boring. Plus, it did the trick. When cross-country season rolled around just days after I got back to Amherst, I was ready to go.

12.
ARHSXC

"A-R-H-S, ARE WE GONNA win? Yes!"

Despite the personal challenges I was facing, running for Amherst Regional High School Cross Country, the "Hurricanes," and my experiences on the team were some of the best days of my life. One of the things I missed most when I went on to run at both Duke and UMass was the camaraderie that the Amherst team built. We took care of each other and had bonds stronger than most I've experienced outside of family. I received outstanding instruction under our head coach, Mr. Keene, and our assistant coach and former ARHSXC runner herself, Alison Wade.

I have heard that many people with eating disorders are obsessed with exercise. Running truly fueled my anorexia. I absolutely *loved* running. It never felt like a chore to me, and I wanted to eat just enough so I could run very well. In fact, on days I had big races or hard workouts coming up, I had no problem eating more as long as I was going to run well. During practice, I wasn't concerned about restricting calories that night or what I was going to eat the next day. In fact, running was not usually about burning more calories or a method to achieve a certain weight. My focus was on being the best runner I could be.

Our high school team had a record book that included a wide variety of records such as standard fastest times, closest split between top runners, and team wins. But it also included more obscure categories, like highest number of different team members to win a race in a season, fastest combined time of sisters on a course, and biggest improvement over a season. Mr. Keene encouraged us to see each member as a contributing factor to the team. Some were obvious scorers – the varsity runners that helped us place well in races. Others exuded motivation. They were the ones who were always positive, helped cheer everyone on, and brought others up around them during workouts, dragging those who were tired along at a faster pace. These runners got "Spirit of the Sport" awards. Others who showed heart and dedication got "Iron Woman" awards for not missing any practices or meets. Because all of us were taught that we were important, everyone felt bonded to the team. We knew we needed each of us to be our best at whatever we were best at.

It is a wonderful feeling to be part of something much larger than yourself. The team at Amherst Regional High School was a close-knit group of girls who might as well have been sisters. Our team had a lot of rituals, from singing a team song before each race to meditating on our backs in a circle. We also had locker buddies – someone we were paired up with at the beginning of the season and for whom we secretly made inspirational signs, notes, and banners before races. It was a tradition that I loved, given my artsy background and devotion to the sport. We also gathered together for pasta dinners before meets and for post-race parties. There were always fun things going on. What's more, with a team of 30 to 40 runners, we constantly had a friendly face to pass in the hallway, a friend with the same lunch period, or someone to catch up with between classes.

Mr. Keene fostered an optimal blend of fun and seriousness. He taught us life skills, ways to be an effective leader, and the importance of building community. He imparted these values in his position as head cross-country coach of the Amherst Girls Team for over ten years. Together with Alison, his coaching experience gave him a good blend of understanding the emotional needs of high school girls and our physical capabilities. Our practices were the right balance of challenging workouts, relatively high mileage for high school girls, and fun easy days with creative themed runs such as mud runs, scavenger hunt runs, or disposable camera runs.

Alison would accompany us on runs, and was the perfect mix of an accomplished, experienced runner who could offer wisdom and advice, and a friend to join in on conversation during practices. It felt like we had an invaluable resource right there beside us, someone able to share insight on racing tactics and overcoming nerves, who could also transmit our concerns and interests back to Mr. Keene.

Mr. Keene knew how to motivate us to work together during practices and races so that, in his words, our "collective achievement was greater than the sum of our individual parts." He taught us to visualize our success through meditation. He encouraged us to use the strength of others on our team when we were struggling. All of his philosophies were important components of a championship team – things that helped us win out over our competition. In my four years of high school, we won the State Championship race three years and placed second the other year.

During my early years of high school, my bedroom became a shrine to the sport of running. I cut out inspirational advertisements, photos, and quotes from magazines and taped them on my wall. "Shoot for the moon. Even if you miss, you'll land among the stars." I put up photos from the team, hung all my medals and ribbons on my closet door, and filled my top bookshelf with trophies. Goals were written on index cards, taped up where I could see them.

By the time I was a junior, my anorexia had become so severe that I was weak and depleted from the chronic lack of calories. I did not always have the necessary strength to push my body through a structured workout such as track intervals, a tempo run, or explosive hill repeats. Sometimes all I could muster was a distance run, with the hope of pushing the pace. Mr. Keene had me do workouts within many of the races because we had dual meets so frequently (perhaps twice per week), where our team easily beat the competition. He was very progressive in his coaching for these races, holding varsity runners back so they weren't pushing an all-out effort several times per week.

Sometimes we paced slower runners on our team so that they might achieve a personal record or win for the season with our help. Other times, as was often the case for me, Mr. Keene would design a workout for me to complete on the course during the race, such as one mile hard, second mile easy, third mile hardest. During races, it was easier for me to pull out a hard effort from my weakened body. One time I was doing mile repeats over at the local college and my heart felt like it was skipping beats. After that, I was pretty scared to try to push it, unless I was racing.

Invitationals were the big races – the days to go for it. I loved these events. They were essentially trips with your best friends to do your favorite thing. Sure, I got very nervous, but the experience was what I trained for. I almost always ran well in races in my early years of high school. I was born tough. It was in my mind to be determined, in my body to be strong, and in my heart to always give it my all. In eighth grade, I started winning some of the dual meets in both cross-country and track, and from then on, I basically expected to be in the top finishers (and I think other people expected this of me as well). These expectations, mine as well as others – teammates, coaches, parents, and teammates' parents – are largely what made me nervous before races. I did not want to let anyone down, especially myself.

The first big race that I won was the freshman race at the Footlocker Northeast Regional Meet at Van Cortland Park in New York City. The freshman race and the seeded race are the two bigger races of the day, although there are separate races for each class year in high school. The race draws runners from all over the Northeast region of the United States, with the top eight places in the seeded race advancing to the National Championships. (They have since changed the qualification process and weight of this race with the advent of the Nike Team Nationals).

I ran the freshman race like a champion. I went out hard, and after the initial half-mile or so of passing runners (I never went out the fastest in races), I moved up into third place for the first mile, and quickly passed another girl for second place. There is a bridge on the course where runners cross into the "backwoods" section. Soon after we crossed the bridge and veered right up a hill, I passed the first-place runner to lead the race. I led the rest of the way with pride, as if it was my duty to lead the other runners.

Being a girl who loved running in the woods and who had pretty severe ADHD, somewhere in those backwoods, I lost the racing mentality. It's not that I stopped trying – I was running fast – but I stopped really pushing and racing. The woods were so beautiful. The hills were rolling, and it felt like I was a car on a roller coaster. I played with the pace, charging the uphills and coasting on the downhills. I enjoyed the crunch of the cinder under my feet and watching the leaves flutter to the ground with each wind gust. I was basically a kid on a playground.

In the final six hundred meters or so, runners re-enter the initial field and run along a cinder path to the finish. It is a long stretch. I took my lead at this point in a somewhat cavalier fashion and started waving to my friends and family, so happy and proud. In the final one hundred meters, the crowds were going wild. Listening intently, I realized they weren't cheering my name, but someone named Daisy. *Someone is behind me!* I started sprinting and eked out my win.

The Footlocker race taught me a few things: I was a great runner, especially for my age, I should enjoy the race experience but stay tough and focused, and finally, I should not count my chickens before they hatched in any race, even if it did seem clear I was going to win. I got a positive and negative reality check – I was a better runner than I even believed I was, and I had to have better control over my ADHD during races. I needed to focus to be my best. I could have fun, but to achieve my potential, I had to remember what the goal was.

Our high school team focused on goal setting. From the very beginning of each season, Mr. Keene would verbalize team goals he had for us, for both the whole season and for individual races and practices. He conducted goal-setting exercises for us to write down our own short- and long-term goals on what we called "power cards." The cards were posted in visible places we encountered on a daily basis as a constant reminder of what we were striving for. Back then, I was very invested in my mental training, and the entire week leading up to the State Championships my sophomore and junior years, I carried my power card on a neck lanyard under my shirt everywhere I went. While I no longer take such extreme measures, I think the mental training was the most useful tool Mr. Keene taught me, and I have relied on these skills long after graduating.

13.
Nora & Mary

I DID NOT HAVE a true "rival" in high school. There were occasionally runners who I knew would be my biggest competition, but we did not race against any teams frequently enough with a challenger for me to really have a rival. I don't mean that in a boastful way, it's just that Amherst dominated the Western Massachusetts running scene in both track and cross-country during my years in high school, and there were not many other runners to push me on opposing teams. The closest things I had to rivals were girls on my own team.

As a freshman on the cross-country team, I had two older teammates to run with – Nora, a junior, and Mary, a senior. They had been training together for two years and seemed somewhat challenged or intimidated by my arrival on the team. For the first few weeks, I felt like an outcast. We would embark on runs where I had no idea where we were going (because routes were named after one of the streets or landmarks, but meant nothing to me). The two of them ran side-by-side on the sidewalk with me stuck behind, trailing like a little dog. From behind, I could not hear their conversations over the sound of the cars—not that I was included in them anyway. It wasn't trailing because I was slower, but I didn't know where we were going, so I couldn't lead. When I would try to run alongside them, I'd "accidentally" get elbowed off the curb.

During races, I usually ended up in third. Something in my mind held me back from truly pushing for anything better. But one day, I beat Mary. She seemed slower than normal for some reason, and my body ached to run faster, feeling like some instinct kept me from passing her. I decided to ignore it and surge ahead. I felt guilty for breaking our tacit agreement of finishing order, but it was what I had to do. I was striving to be the best I could be. The defeat broke Mary somewhat, and after that, I beat her in nearly all of the remainder of that season's races and timed workouts.

Even so, I started to win over their hearts. It was slow, but they began inviting me to run with them on weekends. My mom would drop me off, saying, "Good luck, champ! Don't let them push you around. You've earned your spot too." *She's right. I deserve this too.* I began coming out of my shell – showing my sense of humor, sharing my stories, and asking questions. Within a few weeks, it felt like we were great friends. I was welcomed in.

Running with the two of them became a dream come true. I loved having girls who seemed as invested in improving as I was. They pushed me; I pushed them. We also talked and laughed, explored new trails, and complained together about the workouts. They grew to be my closest friends. Even outside of running, when we passed at school, Nora would run up and hug me or Mary would come over to my locker to say hi, even though I was a freshman and she was a senior.

One race I will never forget was the State Championships my freshman year. It was held in Grafton, on a rough golf course that was part of the Tufts University property. Toeing the line, I was very nervous. I had never run such an important race filled with so many fast runners. When the gun went off, we ran as if in slow motion, the waves of other teams charging ahead of us. We settled in the back quarter of the pack over the first half-mile. Everyone seemed to be faster than us. I was right with Nora and Mary, we were just not near the front. This was very unusual for us, as we were dominant in all of our races in the western region of the state. Another half-mile went by. *Get in this, Am.*

A small little freshman, with just a white long underwear top under my singlet against the cold November morning's chill, I pressed forward. I started passing big waves of runners in one surge, settling in for a minute, and then regaining steam and passing another group. I couldn't see Nora or Mary – I was leading, but I hoped they were following. Mr. Keene looked me in the eye with 600m to go. "Amber, you've got this. Keep going. This is a perfect race."

I kept pushing, tired from my efforts. At this point I was in the top ten, with the winner probably close to finishing. I crested a small hill before the course wound down its last quarter-mile grassy turn into the finish. Nora and Mary surrounded me. "You're almost there, Am." Part of me was mad that they were blowing by me – after all, I was the one that had taken control of this race and led our comeback, but the truth is, I felt relaxed. *They followed! Let them bring it home.* I tried to hang on. Mary sped ahead; I ran next to Nora. In the last straightaway, I pushed my body to sprint. I got sixth in 19:19, right between the fifth and seventh place finishes of Mary and Nora, respectively. I finished first out of all the freshmen in the state.

Exhausted, I pushed my arm up triumphantly into the air in the recovery chute. *I did it!* Our teammates who hadn't run surrounded me, helping to hold me up as my legs begged for me to sit. "What a gutsy race, Sayer," Mr. Keene said as he jogged over. "Real gutsy." We beat out Barnstable High School for the State Title. Amherst runners placed better than in any previous state meet. I was praised for my initiation and competitiveness that ignited our team to take charge of the race.

At the end of the year, Mary graduated, leaving a hole in our training group. The following year, we were occasionally accompanied by the new standout freshman, Spring, but Nora and I usually ran alone together, or joined the boys' group and ran with them. Nora and I formed an even tighter bond, and she became my best friend, a mentor about life, and a companion. I beat her in many races; we had a silent rivalry when the gun went off. My dad, who always cheered secret words we prearranged depending on how close Nora and I were to one another in a race, would cup his hands over his mouth, squat down to be at my ear level, and say "Utah!", which meant I was ahead by about ten meters.

14.
Photo Finish

DURING THE OUTDOOR TRACK season in my freshman year of high school, I was predominantly a miler. This meant that in many of the small races, I ran a variety of distance events, but during the championship season, I focused on the mile. This relatively short event was not my personal strength, but it made strategic sense for the team so we could spread strong runners in all the distance races. I was better suited for the two-mile, because I lacked the raw speed that is advantageous for a miler, but we already had two strong runners who had seniority over me in the two-mile spots.

There are three specific things that are important about the Western Massachusetts Championships outdoor track meet: I narrowly missed qualifying for the State Championships, I saw in action something that became an important goal for me, and I learned how to pick myself up and dust myself off.

That outdoor track season, I probably ran the mile race a dozen times – always within the same few seconds. 5:24, 5:25 – 5:21 was my best, but it was always right around 5:24. Time and time again, big meet or small race, spikes or sneakers, windy or calm, I kept hitting the same time within two or three seconds. This was unbelievable to me, and also frustrating. I just couldn't seem to drop that time down and break 5:20.

I'd like to say that this finally changed at the Western Mass Championships. Standing on the line, I remember being very nervous. I knew the race was going to go out fast (not a tactic I have ever liked), and I really wanted to do well. It all came down to a final lean across the finish line, and I did not have the edge. I ended up in third place by just two one-hundredths of a second – which, in a high school girls' mile race, is very, very close. I had missed qualifying for States by just a lean – in a distance event. I differentiate the event specifically, because this is a relatively large amount of time in a short sprint, where proportionally, it represents a larger amount of the race time, and runners are moving so fast in sprints that every fraction of a second can be some significant distance. In Western Massachusetts, the girls' mile is generally not a highly competitive "down to the tape" race. I ran 5:24.94. I was devastated.

The other important thing that happened during that meet was in an event I was watching, not running. A girl named Jenn Campbell, who ran the Division II (smaller schools) girls' two-mile race, broke 11 minutes, running 10:59.75. I thought that was the coolest thing I had ever watched. She ran two miles in 5:30 pace in a row. I had just run one slightly faster than that. I was in awe. I said out loud, "That is amazing! I want to do that next year."

I took the devastation of not qualifying for states, not improving my time in the mile, and seeing an impressive sub-eleven two-mile as motivation to do better the following year. The rest of the meet, I cheered my teammates, and I even ran in the 4x800 – but my mind was already dreaming of next year, imagining how I could improve, and envisioning what the success would feel like. I even practiced leaning with Matt Lacey, a varsity runner on the boys' team. Matt proved to be a very good friend over the long term as well.

There is a very beautiful picture that was published in our local paper from the race of Matt consoling me with a hug after my race disappointment. The photo reminds me of his friendship, his support of my running, and the lessons I learned that day. I was fired up for sophomore year and this desire fueled my training, ultimately pushing me into a much better runner for the next school year – and yes, my sophomore year I ran the two-mile at the Western Mass Championships. I won in 10:48 – my first time going under the eleven-minute barrier, and running two consecutive 5:24s.

15.
Zeroed Out

AS EARLY AS SEVENTH grade, I developed a variety of tactics to appear to weigh more than I actually did. I'm not going to "advertise" many of these unhealthy habits, but it fills me with tremendous guilt that I was lying every time I stood on the scale. I learned that one gallon of water weighed eight pounds. I would repeat that figure in my head while I forced myself to chug water before a weigh-in, as my body tried to rebel. Water would come up; my eyes would tear.

One particular time, I drank so much water before getting weighed that I became dizzy, nauseous, and was scared to be alone. Standing in my bedroom, my belly distended from two gallons of water, I started seeing stars. I have since learned about hyponeutremia, and that I was probably near coma. I started peeing on the floor uncontrollably. I was actually relieved when my mom came down the hall to weigh me, because I didn't want to be alone. I knew I had screwed myself up. Although I "passed" my weigh-in, I felt so sick during the early class periods at school that day. I remember sitting in Anatomy & Physiology class, and my head was thumping. I couldn't even read the text in my book because my eyesight was so blurred, and my ears felt like they were plugged up. It hurt to walk around because I was so bloated with water, and I was thankful every time I went to the bathroom that I could breathe a little better. I swore to myself that I needed to get better.

Looking back, it's hard to not want to grab myself and shake some sense into that tiny little body. There were short epiphanies where I scared sense into myself for a minute or two. One such time involved my favorite pair of pants. They weren't jeans, but they were blue cotton pants from the Gap, girls' size 8, that we got at a tag sale. I remember putting them on at the beginning of my junior year of high school after a summer of wearing shorts, only to find that they fell all the way down my hips, settling in a heap around my ankles. *Shit. When did I get thinner?* I'd briefly agree in my head with the voices of various adults telling me I needed help, only to have the voraciousness of the disease take over my brain again later that same day, wanting to keep my body thin at all costs.

When my parents started weighing me regularly, they bought a standard spring-loaded bathroom scale – the kind you stand on and the dial spins and points to your weight. I learned how to adjust the zeroing out of the scale, so I had it set to read a few pounds of weight when nothing was even on it. When weighing time came, as long as I either stepped on quickly before they had time to check that it was at zero, or I picked it up and the needle was moving around when I stepped on it, they had no idea. Then I would stay standing on it until they left, or simply pick it up and hold it until they left. Incrementally, I would move the zeroing balance so that initially, I was only cheating by two or three pounds, but eventually it must have been close to ten pounds.

When we arrived to music camp in Maine before my sophomore year, I was shocked to be weighed and measured by the camp nurse at the initial check-in day in front of my parents. There was no way to cheat. In clothes and shoes, I was about nine pounds lighter than they thought I was. "The scale must be wrong!" they reasoned. I was relieved I had gotten away with it. This relief was short-lived. When my parents got home and saw my home scale (that I had forgotten to adjust back to normal) they freaked out. It was probably one of the days I was in the most trouble. It was almost lucky that I was going to be away from them at the sleepover camp for four whole weeks. I did have to weigh-in once a week at camp, but that was a minor obstacle.

I must say, I remember really not enjoying myself at camp because I was worried that my parents were not going to let me run cross-country. Not only was I significantly lighter than they thought, I had also been dishonest by cheating the system. Needless to say, they invested in a digital scale and I had to rethink how I could get by.

Another issue was that I unconsciously began spinning a web of lies to get around eating, or to get in a run. To this day, that aspect still really stings me to admit that I was such a low, dishonest person. I am filled with incredible guilt; I am disgusted by my deceitfulness. To avoid eating more, I would say that I was going to eat out with friends - and then when I met up with them, I'd say I ate at home.

One time in eighth grade when I was "not allowed" to run, according to my parents, I ran quickly around the block a few times after school because I knew my parents would be working late and I'd have enough time. As soon as I was back inside the front door, my dad pulled into the driveway. *Oh no!* I raced upstairs and took off my sweaty running clothes, then ran with my school clothes to the bathroom. "Ambs? You home?" Dad yelled. "One minute, Dad, I'm in the bathroom." I tried to fluff up my sweaty, matted hair. My face was flushed, and I was still sweating. I heard him coming up the stairs as I vigorously dried my hair with my towel. When I came out, he blinked at me irritably and said, "You look all sweaty."

"Oh, I was just in the bathroom a while, I wasn't feeling well," I said, and thought to myself, *what does that even mean?!* Even today, I laugh at the ridiculousness of that line. Who would rather be embarrassed that they were drenched in sweat after a trip to the bathroom than back from a run?

Then there was the issue of hiding food, or pretending I ate more than I did, both of which are just another form of lying. The best example of this was my ability to avoid drinking most of the infamous "cans," as I called them: a caloric supplement to my diet, required by my pediatrician and enforced by my parents. They were disgustingly thick, calorically dense, Walmart brand nutritional shakes in small 8-ounce cans. I hated them - not just because they had 360 calories and 16 grams of fat, but also because they tasted like hand lotion and had a repulsive texture.

In the two or three years I was "on cans," I probably only drank the full can a few times. One of the exploitable attributes that my devious mind recognized in them was their disgusting thickness. If I didn't shake them up, the viscous gel-like consistency would remain sunk and stuck to the bottom, and a thinner, more liquid solution rose to the top. If I drank that and quickly tipped the can over and back upright, it appeared the can was empty, since the thick sludge was too slow to drip out. I could also accomplish this by vortexing the drink in my hand, so that the thick goop would stick to the can's ridged walls. Other times, I'd open it fast and dump out the majority of the can when no one was looking, then fill the rest up with water and drink. You couldn't see inside, so this was the best tactic. Regardless of the method I chose, I was constantly evading the cans in a deceitful way. It shames me to say that this reprehensible behavior was not isolated to these cans, but extended to other foods and activities as well.

16.
Brown Running Camp

DESPITE RUNNING GENERALLY BEING very effortless when I was younger, there were certainly runs that seemed like insurmountable challenges. The summer after my freshman year of high school, a group of eight girls and eight boys from the Amherst cross-country teams went to a running camp hosted by Brown University in Rhode Island. It was a week of running, running-related games, general camp activities, and hanging out. The food was terrible, but the runs were fun, and it was an unparalleled experience of having a good time with my teammates. My sister, Emily, also came, and in fact, that's where she met the boy who would later become her husband, who ran for the boys' team.

One of the hardest runs I can remember occurred at this camp. We would usually run a few miles before breakfast, and then do a full run later in the afternoon. On one of the afternoon runs, the August sun was beating down. The pavement had heat ripples hovering above it. I was exhausted. I just didn't have it. The guys I usually ran with seemed to have no trouble pushing the pace. They did not seem tired like me. I could not keep up. As I would fall back a little, it would get in my head that I was losing them and doing badly, and then I would fall back further. *Why can't you keep up with them? You should be as good. Why are you so awful today? What happened to you?*

On this particular run, I was lucky that my friend Matt saw me struggling and decided to hang back with me. He could have been running comfortably up with the leaders, pushing the pace, but he cruised back with me, helping the time pass. He talked and told me stories through the miles to keep my mind occupied, and offered encouragement. "You'll get them tomorrow. This is a good pace for today. They are going to be paying the price tomorrow." I felt bad that he was missing out on a harder workout, but he was kind and tried to get me to dismiss that concern. "No. This is great to run with you today. I'll be stronger tomorrow and be able to push when it matters – in the real workout."

Matt helped me tremendously that day. By hanging back and running with me, he kept me focused and positive and able to get through the run. He also taught me that you don't have to "have it" every single run to be great. In fact, it is better to listen to your body. If you need an easy day, slow down and give your body what it needs. If your body wants rest, then pushing too hard for too many days in a row will only lead to total fatigue and poorer performance. He also taught me that it's okay to accept companionship from teammates, because those strong bonds motivate you to race harder since you do not want to let your friends down.

17.
2002 Penn Relays

ON APRIL 1 IN my sophomore year of high school, my track coach, Chris Gould, called me. I remember the day precisely because I was home sick with the stomach flu. I rarely missed school, but this was one of those bugs that kept even me home. If you missed school, you missed practice, and that always motivated me to make sure I went to school, even if I felt a little sick. I was academically inclined, so it's not that I wanted to miss school, but when my parents would try to keep me home if I was a little under the weather, I would push to go in. It was one of the last few years we had a house phone and it was rare that I picked it up, but I felt lonely in the house by myself, so I answered.

Mr. Gould informed me that my times during the season had qualified me to run the individual 3,000-meter run (about two miles) at the Penn Relays, which would be held just a few weeks later. He was also going to be taking the boys 4x800m relay, and wanted to know if that was something I would be interested in. "Are you kidding me?! I'm in!" When I got off the phone, I pushed my vomit bucket aside, got out of my bed, and in the middle of my bedroom, threw one fist into the air triumphantly. "YES!"

My race was on a Thursday night, and the boys were racing Friday morning. We were going to stay at Mr. Gould's brother's house outside of Philadelphia in New Jersey. We left Thursday afternoon from school, which soon proved to be too late. By the time we reached the sprawl of traffic outside Philadelphia five hours later, there was not much time left before my race. We still needed to check in, pick up my race number, and get me to the starting line. Penn Relays is one of those races where runners are required to be in their "pens" well before the start of the race, so that groups can efficiently get on the track, run, and clear the track for the next event. There are so many heats of races that happen in a day that officials need operations to run as smoothly and quickly as possible. This is accomplished in part by making sure all runners report to their group on the track well before the race.

We finally got to the race registration where we needed to pick up our packet with my number, but everyone was gone. A volunteer still on the premises said that registration was over and that packets were no longer available. My coach was a fighter, and I knew that he could get me my number. He instructed me to go warm up and not to worry. He would get the packet. On top of my normal anxiety before a race, my adrenaline was really pumping with the stress of the traffic, the fear I was not going to be permitted to run after setting my heart on it, and the knowledge that this race would be in front of so many spectators.

As I ran around the campus, I heard the final announcement on the loud speaker for my race. I rushed back to the track, but could not figure out how to get in the gated walls. I ran around to the back of the stadium where we had arrived. Vendors selling cotton candy, soft pretzels, and sodas were drawing large crowds. I tried to slip through the crowd and make my way to the stadium entrance. Breathlessly, I ran up to a guard. "I need to get in there. They made the final call for my race." "Where's your pass?" *My pass!? I didn't have one!* That's what Mr. Gould was trying to track down for me. I explained the situation, and just as the guard was about to deny me access, Mr. Gould came pushing through the same crowd to find me. "Got it! Go get 'em."

The remainder of the time before the race was spent cooped up in the pen with the other 3,000-meter runners, trying to get my heart rate to slow down from the pre-race panic. Since I had missed an opportunity for a proper warm-up, I jogged along part of the stadium they had fenced off for runners, before another racer and I were reprimanded for not staying put in our pen. With the sun down, it was cool. A chill moved through my thin body. Anxious and excited, I looked up in the stands and found the familiar faces of my coach and the five boys who had come to run the 4x8 (one was an alternate). They waved excitedly. *Breathe, Am, you can do this.*

We lined up in order of our seed, with runners with the fastest qualifying times assigned the lowest seed numbers. Since I had just eked under the qualifying time, I was seeded last. My starting position was furthest out on a waterfall start (in short, not an ideal position). When the gun went off, I turned into the racer that I was. I hung in the back for the first three or four laps, which is harder than it sounds. Racers are inclined to go out hard, and generally if you are in the back, you are not doing well. Because I was accustomed to leading races at this point, this was an uncomfortable position for me. With that said, the race went out faster than any two-mile I had ever run, and even hanging on at the end for dear life, I was hitting faster splits than I had planned on. "Perfect pace, Amber. Stay right in there." Mr. Gould's reassurance helped me remain calm.

As the laps went on, I started passing runners. I ended up getting eighth place with a major personal record of 10:12.57, lobbing nearly thirty seconds off my previous best. I was thrilled. That night I cooled down after the race with a girl I had become close with through the Massachusetts racing circuit, a junior named Sara. She had run the girls' mile just before me. We ran through the streets of Philadelphia. I felt so grown up, running in an unknown city after a great race. Turns out we were overzealous on our cool-down and got lost in the city. We ran for nearly an hour more than Mr. Gould expected, worrying him sick, but I was so happy.

That night I couldn't sleep. I lay on the floor of a baby's room waiting for sleep to come. I was too wound up from the late night effort. But I smiled because I was proud, and because I felt so excited for the remainder of the track season.

18.
Center Stage Behind the Register

THE DAY AFTER I turned sixteen was halfway through the summer between my sophomore and junior years of high school. In Massachusetts, this is the age where you can work legally without permits. I had wanted a job for some time and had an "in" through my friend Nick on the boys' cross-country team, who worked at the local store, A.J. Hastings, in the center of Amherst. I interviewed, and due to the glowing recommendation Nick gave me, I was offered the job on the spot. My starting shifts were opening Sunday morning (6 a.m. -12 p.m.) and one night a week (5 - 9 p.m.).

Perhaps more so than the typical "first job," my job at Hastings ultimately became a huge part of my life. I worked there for the better part of seven years, lived with my bosses for several months at one point in college, and began my lifelong relationship with Ben, who I later married.

Hastings put me in the spotlight of our little town. I was the superstar. Most of the customers learned my name. Newspaper clippings of my successes were taped up on the walls, and some "regulars" would ask me to recap the races during my Sunday shift. I enjoyed feeling like I had "fans" and people who wanted to hear about my running. Customers asked me about injuries, talked about their own fitness routines, and predicted my finish times. I received good-luck cards and was even asked to sign a few newspaper photos of myself. None of my fans ever mentioned that I was super skinny, asked if I had an eating disorder, or made me feel like anything other than an elite runner. I liked that all of my coworkers accepted me and assumed I was so thin because I ran competitively, and I also genuinely enjoyed the job. It made me feel "grown up" and more in charge of my life.

During my battle with anorexia, one of the things I loved about Hastings was that it gave me the freedom to be more active, as well as eat less. It was a perfect way to avoid eating. My mom often brought me dinner food if I came right after practice, and I'd pick at it after she left, reporting that I ate it all. On Sundays, sometimes I would pretend I was working until 1:00pm instead of noon and go running right after work. Then I'd run yet again later in the afternoon from home, under the guise that it was my first run of the day.

19.
"Superstitions are habits rather than beliefs."

- Marlene Dietrich

IT'S NOT UNCOMMON FOR runners to have superstitious behaviors or "lucky" charms on race day. Sometimes this constitutes a certain meal they must eat the night before or the morning of the race, a particular pair of lucky socks they must race in, or special laces for their spikes. These habits form because routine helps to keep racing a little more relaxing. The more elements you are accustomed to, the fewer variables you are leaving to chance on a stressful day when you are trying to run fast. Over the years, I developed a few of these rituals.

For some time, I had a "lucky" bra and socks I liked to wear, but those eventually lost significance when I raced better in something different. When it was a big important race, my mom would French braid two braids in the back of my hair. I loved this, mainly because I enjoyed spending time with her before the race. While she would do my hair, I would gab on and on about who my competition was going to be, what I was nervous about, the challenges of the course, and my goals. Mom was a great listener and calmed my nerves. When I had the braids, I knew it meant, "Go big or go home."

Since about age eight, I had wanted a GameBoy, but my parents never got me one. At one point in fifth grade, in my *Kids Discover* magazine, there was a sweepstakes for a GameBoy. It said to fill out the enclosed sweepstakes card and mail it in the envelope in the centerfold of the magazine. Specially marked and coded entry cards and envelopes would win a brand new Nintendo GameBoy and various games. As I was still at the age when I believed I could do anything, I was sure that my envelope was a winner. The reason: it was green. In my mind, all of the other kids had normal white envelopes. It was clear to me that with green, I was special, destined to win. Who uses green envelopes?

The small print after the sweepstakes rules included information about the odds of winning, which I ignored, and the little line that said, "Please allow six weeks for delivery upon sweepstakes deadline," which I seemed to forget about. Every day when the bus dropped me off at the end of our road, I grasped my backpack straps at my chest and ran all the way to the mailbox, hoping to find my GameBoy inside. This went on for quite some time, beginning the day I mailed in the entry, until the end of the school year in June – probably a good eight weeks. The GameBoy never came; I never won. The normal reaction to this would have probably been, "I guess I didn't win. Green must not have been lucky after all." However, my thinking was, "I bet my entry got lost in the mail, or they couldn't send me the GameBoy because they needed to give it to someone in a wheelchair." (As a young child, I was unusually obsessed with individuals with disabilities.)

My desire to own a GameBoy continued long past elementary school. On an April afternoon of eighth grade, I sat in my school's auditorium with the other members of my class. A marketing crew came on the stage and announced that we would be participating in a magazine sale to fundraise for our end-of-the-year trip. Volunteers began passing out colorful, glossy packets about the magazine choices and the incentive prizes students could earn if we achieved certain quotas. There it was: eight subscriptions earned the seller a portable Tetris Game. It was the closest to owning a GameBoy I had come since fifth grade. Even though it was not a real GameBoy, I decided it would suffice. I scribbled a list in my notebook detailing everyone I could possibly think of who would buy a subscription from me. I was accustomed to selling, due to years of pushing Girl Scout Cookies, so I managed to get eight buyers. About two months later, my portable Tetris Game arrived.

My best friend on the boy's team was James. We were in the same class and had been friendly growing up, becoming good friends in seventh grade when we started running together. We were both hired by Hastings on the same day and took over the early Sunday morning shift together there. When we started, neither of us could drive, so we would meet on our bikes halfway between our houses at 5:20 in the morning to head "uptown" (the center of Amherst is at the top of a hill) to work together. Since James is nearly a year older than me, he got his license before me and would come to pick me up in the morning once he was able to drive.

Sunday mornings, we had a routine. We would assemble newspapers and talk about the previous day's race: aspects that went well, what we were disappointed with, goals for the next race. We would read all the coverage in the local papers as we stuffed them. Over time, we became close friends, bonding in our hopes to improve our running, and in our dream of winning States together.

Before races, James and I would play the Tetris Game. We happened to play it before one race, and it quickly became a tradition for the two of us and our friend Ian, one grade older than us. I simply wanted to pass the time driving to a track meet on a long, otherwise boring bus ride. For someone with ADHD, track meets are much worse than cross-country races. Between the travel to the event and the long schedule of dozens of events and heats in each event, it is usually an all-day affair. Sometimes having something to do between watching races and competing in your events is necessary.

The three of us had a little rivalry built into our superstitious participation with the Tetris Game. Whoever scored highest in the game would have the best race. We would alternate who got to keep the game at home to practice in between meets, where we would compete for the highest score. We got so good that on the two-hour ride from Amherst to Boston, sometimes only two people would get the chance to go, because the games lasted so long without the player losing.

20.
"Finding Joe"

THE SUMMER BETWEEN MY sophomore and junior years of high
school, I attended a running camp at Dartmouth College in
Hanover, New Hampshire. New England has many running
camps, but I chose this particular one because Dartmouth was a
school I was potentially interested in attending. I figured it would
be a good way to meet the coaches, make an impression, and get a
sense of what it might be like to be a student athlete there. I
remember feeling very grown-up because we lived in the dorms (I
had a single), and we got meal cards to eat in the dining hall like
real students.

The camp actually got off to a very rocky start for me, because
the directors placed me in the top girls' group. However, I was
much faster than the other girls at the camp. The coaches'
philosophy was that boys and girls should be in separate groups
because it could create "unhealthy competition" or low self-esteem
(not a philosophy I subscribed to). Thankfully, after calling my
parents and asking them to beg the coaches to let me switch
groups, I was placed in an appropriately-paced group. My parents
were fine executing this request because they had paid for me to
have a good week of training, to learn more about the sport, and
to get some value out of the camp. The director hemmed and
hawed with my dad, who was never the type to back down easily,
and let me upgrade a few groups so that I was pace-matched, rather
than sex-matched.

My new group was mostly welcoming, and I was used to
running with boys because our track team ran integrated under the
guidance of Chris Gould. Some ten years later, I can't remember
the names of the other campers. However, my group leader

counselor, Joe McKnight, changed my life. Joe was a former Dartmouth runner who had graduated a few years prior to the camp. I was so grateful that he happily welcomed me to the group and treated me like his other runners.

Joe made me feel special. He had a way of connecting with me that few people had been able to up to that point in my life. When he spoke to me, I listened, and while this in and of itself was not highly uncommon for me, he reached me with positive words. When he complimented me, it had an authenticity that other people seemed to lack. He made me believe I was worth something. Yes, I was a good runner, and he certainly built up my ego regarding that, but he touched me with our conversations about how he thought I was a good person – a special type, one of those real gems in a population.

The time at camp under Joe's leadership improved my self-esteem by leaps and bounds, not just as an athlete (I was often doubting my ability before races), but also as a person. It is hard to explain how certain people impact you because it is so rare that, unless you have experienced it, it cannot really be equated to anything else.

Joe and I remained in touch after the camp had finished. We emailed back and forth about everyday life, how my cross-country season was going, how he was doing, and then eventually going into other aspects of our lives – family, life goals, fears, good and bad things going on. Joe proved to be the best listener in my life. For the first time, it felt like someone truly wanted to understand me. This felt so unique to me – which, in hindsight, truly breaks my heart.

Joe was incredibly compassionate and wise beyond his years. I saved many of his emails, and now that I am older than he was at the time, I can confirm that he was quite wise for his age. We did not talk about easy things, but he was so non-judgmental and offered nothing but love, understanding, any advice he had, and hopeful words. Joe made me feel like I had something to offer other people and the world. He helped me see value in myself, to view bad things in a more positive light, and to relish in my accomplishments and the good things. He taught me that I was worth listening to. That aspect of our relationship had the biggest impact on my life. I knew that someone thought I mattered, no matter how well I ran, how I was struggling with weight, or how much it felt like my parents hated me.

Joe and I never talked explicitly about the fact that I was anorexic, although he was the first person that I came close to admitting it to without directly using the words. He knew, and he still cared about me. He just wanted me to get better and be happy.

Below is an email exchange between us that took place shortly after camp that broaches the subject of my eating disorder, after my parents barred me from running one weekend:

9/11/02

Joe –

First of all I am just wondering if you have AOL instant messenger so that i could talk to you on that sometimes if you did. Secondly, and again I dont have nearly the time I want to write to you, but I will try to explain a little bit about what is going on as akward and uncomfortable and impersonal as it may feel through email.

Well I cant remember what all I told you in my last brief message, but basically things have fallen apart and I have hit rock bottom. This weekend was the lowest time for me emotionally in probably just about my whole life. I dont think there was a continuous stretch lasting over 20 minutes in which I didnt cry. I cried the whole weekend. Basically my parents were really mad at me for being so depressed and not talking to them about it. They said I was using running to alieviate my problems (which does hold some truth) and that I could no longer run. Then they said I could no longer work because I enjoyed escaping my reality while being away in another setting and that school couldnt be a priority. They said I had to gain 12 pounds and make friends, and they said they were going to hospitalize me for 6 weeks in Brattleboro or something. I was under room arrest the whole weekend which entailed me under the watchful eye of one parent the whole weekend, not one time out of the house, absolutely no running, phone conversations, or personal space, no writing in my journal, and escorts to even the bathroom -oh and TONS and TONS of food. And every time I cried I got yelled at. The dynamic within the room was so tense and for me ineffably upsetting. I was so scared and so alone seriously all I wanted to do was die and I had cried so much I just felt so sick and headachy and lost.

My parents fought a lot about what was going on with them and with me, because a lot of this has to do with issues they have between themselves regarding me. I did return to school today but am still under their watchful, critical, unloving eyes when I return. And my coach called and made them let me run since we had a dual meet today so I just did a little workout on the course during the race, but my head wasnt in it (although I think that's understandable) and it was also had to focus during school. I talked to one of my best friends who has gone off to college though and he reminded me of the strength I possess and that I just need to be tough and although I might not find any love or support or understanding here at home, there are a couple of people like himself who care about me and for them I must keep going. With that I felt a little lifted and I'm seriously just trying to take things one day at a time, keep my head level and find some good in something everyday if I cant find it within myself. I'm just starting to hate myself and feel very sad. I feel like I just told you a lot I probably shouldnt, but I guess at this point, you are one of the very few people who doesnt treat me and what I say critically, gives me the time of day to care about what I say, and I know you'll just listen and I can trust you for that. Hope you've been doing well. I promise I'll try to send more uplifting messages along as soon as I can. I hope we are still friends Lord knows i need you!

Amber

To which he replied:

9/13/02

Amber,

Let me first apologize~i don't have aol messenger. I know that is the new young thing to have, but i don't have it yet. sorry. if i ever get one though, you will be the first to know. promise!!

Have your parents let you run, since you wrote this? I certainly hope this. a runner needs running like humans and animals need air and food. What's the situation? I don't know really what to say this time. I didn't have any idea all the things you were dealing with. I knew you were dealing witha lot, but I didn't know it was THIS MUCH. You are too young to feel so low and deal with so much. This is not very fair, in my opinion—yours too, I assume. Amber, Amber, Amber...

What can I say? Are you going to go to Brattleboro? Do you have an eating disorder? That is what your e-mail implied. Is it the truth?~you don't have to tell me, but I'm telling you that you can. It isn't something I would ever tell, nor is it something I would ever take advantage of knowing. To understand the situation more, I wouldn't mind knowing. But, you don't have to tell me the truth~you can lie and I won't know the difference. ***(I say this is like the famous "Virgin" question. It seems like virgins always answer "yes, I'm a virgin" and non~virgins always answer "that's private information." which, defeats the purpose of having the option to respond. So, as a friend, I'm ASKING you to lie to me if you are not ready to tell me, or to tell me the truth~whatever you feel comfortably writing, I feel comfortable reading. get what I'm saying? I don't wantto force you, basically, to answer the question)***

Other than that, have you stopped crying? I can't imagine there is enough water in Mass for you to continue like that without rehydrating:) ~poor humor, but i'm trying to make you smile the best i can:)

I don't know your parents and I can't judge them based on your words alone (that would not be fair to them, on my part, DESPITE my desire to be the most sympathetic listener I can be for YOU). However, without being unfair, I can comfortably tell you that I wonder very much what is going on and why there exists such a lack in communication. I simply don't understand it. You are so smart, Amber. The most mentally handicapped person could understand every word you say because you are eloquent. I am baffled by the communication problem that exists between your parents and you. It is so unfortunate because it could be so much more productive than it seems to be, ya know what I mean?

I hate to say this, but I have to go. I have some trips to prepare for and I have to spend some time with extended family members. Just so you know, I am probably going to be out of contact for almost 2 weeks, but I will write again as soon as I am permitted the time. Be good to yourself and please take care of my girl, AMBER.OK?

Peace and love,
Joe

Joe and I communicated frequently over the first year after camp, and then less frequently for the next year after that. There were no bad feelings between us, but our lives were diverging more, as he was several years out of college and into the "real world," and I was busy applying for colleges and moving on from high school.

I reconnected with Joe as I started writing this memoir. I sent him an email hoping it would still get to him, and that he would remember who I was. He amazed me with a loving, excited response. I thanked him for the years of friendship and wisdom that he provided me, which I desperately needed. "You were always a special girl; I just wanted you to feel that," he told me.

21.
Goodbyes

I'VE NEVER BEEN GOOD at goodbyes. Most people aren't, but I wear my heart on my sleeve. I truly feel a sense of loss that often haunts me, occupying my mind completely. Being a particularly demonstrative person, goodbyes often result in me crying. Of course, I've always been very emotional at the loss of loved ones, the moving away of friends, and breakups. But I get emotionally attached to places as well as the ending of experiences. I am a girl of nostalgia.

One goodbye that was particularly hard for me was the end of sophomore year when the bulk of my friends, who had been seniors, graduated. I missed all of them and felt disengaged from a social life when they left, despite having some peers my age that were friends.

22.
Running before Running

As my anorexia ran rampant during my junior year of high school, I felt that cross-country practice frequently did not provide sufficient mileage compared to what I was aiming for. The summer before junior year, I was consistently hitting seventy and eighty miles per week. During that time, I had the flexibility to run however much I could fit in between my part-time job at Hastings and the distance I could sneak in when it was assumed I was not running anymore that day. Some days, I would time runs to start right when my mom was leaving, while pretending I wouldn't be leaving for another half hour or so, so I could run longer. Other times, I would squeeze in a short run while everyone in the house was either on an errand or elsewhere. Basically any time I had the house to myself, I would run, unless I had already hit the mileage I wanted.

When cross-country season rolled around, I no longer had control of my schedule and lost hours of available running time while at school. I wasn't able to run in the morning because my parents were running or otherwise around, or my sister Emily would tattle on me. Nights, like mornings, were not an option. Practice lasted a few hours after school, and in the evening I had oboe lessons, or a shift at Hastings, or I was expected home. The only available time I had was immediately after school, before practice. School ended at 2:20 p.m. and practice started roughly at 3:00. At the beginning of the season, when we were still blessed with ample daylight, practices started as late as 3:15 because our coaches encouraged us to meet after school with teachers if we needed academic help.

As soon as the bell rang, I would rush to the locker room, my mind completely focused on squeezing in as much running as I could to burn calories, train harder, and get better. Everyone would think it was crazy that I was running before practice, so I had to be stealthy and hit the pavement quickly. I could make it from my English class (my last period of the day) to the locker room in under a minute if I was willing to push through the elated students in the hallway who were glad that the day was over. I would be the first one in there and could change in less than a minute, run to the bathroom, and escape through the convenient backdoor of our locker room that opened to the back sports fields. Just as the door would close behind me, I would hear the giggles and the voices of my teammates streaming into the locker room. But I was free.

I would run swiftly in a tangent across the sports fields, trying to avoid any possible teammates that would be on the main paved sidewalks and exits of the school. As soon as I was across the field, I zipped across a little path in someone's backyard that students who walked to school trudged through as a shortcut on their commute. The path emptied out onto the small side street we frequently ran on for our track workout warm-up loops. I could usually get in exactly 30 minutes of running before practice – which, at the speeds I was pushing, was probably a solid 4.5 miles. My loop was secluded. I did not want other runners to see me, or to encounter athletes from other sports teams or their coaches. I stuck to running the trails of our cross-country course backwards, avoiding bus and car traffic. Then I would enter Wildwood Cemetery – a beautiful, wooded cemetery about a mile from the school. I would fit in about two to three miles of various loops, depending on how much time I had, then head back.

Getting back into the school unnoticed was infinitely harder. Most obviously, I was sweaty. I have always perspired significantly, and because it was still the warm temperatures of early fall and I had just banged out nearly five miles, I looked flushed and damp, which I feared would blow my cover. I would sometimes try to quietly enter the same door I exited and go straight to the bathroom. I would buff my sweaty hair as vigorously as possible to dry away excess moisture. I tried to wear colors that minimized sweat in my shirt, but some days I would tiptoe around others still changing to switch into a dry shirt. Because it was usually just minutes before practice started, the locker room tended to be sparse at this time – perfect for me to quickly get back outside, looking as fresh as possible.

Once or twice girls in the locker room asked me if I had already run. "No," I'd say, my heart beginning to accelerate with my dishonesty. "I was just sweating because it's hot out." One day, when I hit the "safety" zone on the other side of the sports fields on the side street, my friend James and a few of his buddies drove up the street. "Running already?" he asked. "Yeah, just a different schedule for me today," I lied, hoping he wouldn't see me half an hour later at practice. Thankfully, because boys and girls practiced separately, I stood a good chance of getting away with it.

Sneaking in runs was not new to me. My best friend on the team and my "partner in crime," Samantha, was just as obsessed with running as I was, even though we ran different paces. She and I hated "fun run" days because they did not provide enough mileage. When we were freshmen and sophomores on the team, sometimes we would sneak out together before practice, just as I would later do myself. We called them "red barn runs" because we would innocently walk to a small red bathroom shed on the school premises, out near the community pool and playground. Once behind the barn, we would slip out of the gated property to the free world and begin running.

Often we ran these runs together, even though we usually did not train together during practice, but I was happy to run at a more leisurely pace to have company on some "bonus" miles. When we finished our short loop (maybe three miles) back at the barn, we went inside to the bathroom to hide evidence of our running (drying our hair and washing our face). Then we would giddily walk back across the football field, as if we were two children that just got into the cookie jar, pretending we were returning from a quick errand in town. This allowed us to enjoy the "fun run" in a more relaxed mindset.

23.
Sisters

MY SISTER EMILY'S FRIENDSHIP my junior year was one of the few that I had left. I had systematically and somewhat unconsciously started to withdraw from my peers and lose my friends that were still in high school with me. I had been emotionally closer to the running friends that graduated and moved on before my junior year. This amounted to a tremendous loss for me.

Emily was willing to talk with me in school. She asked me to sit with her group of friends when we were in the same physics class. On my sixteenth birthday, when I failed to pass my weigh-in, I was grounded. Emily probably looked at my sickly body, disgusted by the damage I had wrought and mad about how much I stressed out our parents. But she was a sister before a hater. She begged our parents to let her take me out for a short, supervised trip to Groff Park. Emily knew I needed some fresh air, and that crying for fifteen hours on my birthday would not be healthy. She sat with me on the swings and told me it was going to be okay. I'm not sure I knew what she meant by "it," but it was a moment where I was blessed that she offered love in my otherwise blanket of tremendous sadness.

Ashleigh and I had a somewhat less strained relationship because she was several years older than me, and therefore out of the house for many of the more severe days of my anorexia. She also suffered from body image issues and disordered eating (although perhaps not a full-blown eating disorder), and therefore I think it was something she felt she should not approach me about, if she wasn't healthy either. In the more recent future with distance between me and my anorexia, we have since talked about it on numerous occasions.

24.
Nice Dress

AS IF IT WERE yesterday, I can clearly recall one afternoon early in the cross-country season my junior year. I dropped my backpack in my car, then crossed the parking lot in front of the school to walk over to practice. I was wearing a light purple tank top, which made me feel "fast" and excited for practice. My mind was fired up for a challenging workout.

Mr. Keene called me over and ushered me into the athletic director's office. I was met by a small group of important adults in my life – the head and assistant athletic directors, my coach, our assistant coach, Alison, the head boys' cross country (and my track) coach, my school guidance counselor, and my parents. The mood was so tense that I lost feeling in my feet as panic overwhelmed my body. They confronted me about my weight, and stated that it was difficult to allow me to continue running cross-country when I was clearly unhealthy.

I felt like I was on trial. I scanned their faces, looking for comfort. My heart began racing; I could feel it beating in my ears. *Can they hear it thumping?* I was petrified that I was going to lose the only thing in my life I really loved, scared that I was going to be forced to eat more, and ultimately terrified that everyone could tell I was anorexic. (I was under the naive impression that people were oblivious to my disease, because I was rarely asked or confronted about it.) We all crafted a very lenient game plan: I would be weighed once a week by my pediatrician, and needed to be cleared each week before I could run. I can see now that the game plan we came up with was not aggressive enough, as it did not curtail my eating disorder.

My weekly weigh-in soon turned into a three-day-per-week event, as I was not putting on weight. On Mondays, Wednesdays, and Fridays, my pediatrician, whom I grew to hate, would weigh me in nothing but a gown. I was treated like a criminal suspect in her office. Even the receptionists always looked at me with disgust, as if to say, "Just eat, shithead. Then you won't have to come here and take up space in my waiting room every other day."

Once inside the exam room, the nurse would watch me undress to make sure that I was not cheating. When my pediatrician entered the room, the appointment continued to run its predicted path. She would wear a black dress with small white polka dots, as she did every single day. She would check the new weight, then sit on her stool, wheel over to me, and say nothing. She'd flip through the last measurements and plot my new weight on the growth chart. With an audible sigh, she'd report, "You're not gaining, Amber." She and my mom would start interrogating me about what my plan was to start gaining weight. I'd throw out the usual: "I just have to eat more this week. I'll add an extra 'can.'" Several times they discussed various inpatient options, threatening that if weight was not gained by the next appointment, I'd be en route to Brattleboro or Boston.

In the car ride back home, Mom would look at me with disdain. The tension in her hands turned her knuckles white against the gray steering wheel. I knew she was thinking, "You're wasting everyone's time doing this three times a week. Just eat, for Christ's sake!" That night, I'd be in the dog house at home, waiting for my mom to share the bad news with my dad, and hoping Emily would act neutral and do her homework next to me. I feel isolated and lonely. I was the ultimate burden – afraid that even my own parents would prefer I was dead.

25.
"You may no longer consider yourself a Hurricane"

HALFWAY THROUGH THE CROSS-COUNTRY season, I broke my foot and I was kicked off of the team. The official removal happened one day after practice. Mr. Keene told my mom that I was no longer part of the team, and that I needed to turn in my uniform. I was not to attend any team functions or interact with teammates, and could not cheer at races, which was especially insulting because Emily was on the team and I loved supporting her. She and I were very close at this point, and she was running well. The expulsion was a shock to my parents, and an even bigger shock to me.

Recently, I was talking with my mom and trying to recall being ousted from the team, because quite frankly, I realized that I was still not sure why I was removed. My mom shared in my confusion. She said that Mr. Keene was in a difficult position having me on the team: I was an extremely talented runner, and honestly at a much higher level than others on our already successful team. Mr. Keene loved winning. Even though I was dangerously thin, he liked having the fastest team possible. As a driven runner, I benefited from this. Where other coaches may have banned me from running until sufficient weight had been gained, Mr. Keene walked the fine line of emphasizing that as long as I was "cleared" by the pediatrician to run, he would welcome me on the team.

While I found ways to cheat my way through my weigh-ins, my running continued to improve, and Mr. Keene was happy to have me as one of his athletes. Somewhat surprisingly, given the intervention that took place earlier in the season, my weight was not the reason I was cut. My mom said Mr. Keene cited me as being "oppositional." I now understand what he meant. My junior year, I was fairly broken down. I was simply not eating enough and had lost measureable weight from my sophomore year. I often did not have the strength to do structured workouts, because if I happened to not run well because I was too weak, it would go to my head, causing me to get down on myself and feel like I was no longer fast (yes, I am a bit of a head case).

Also by this time, I had a firm grasp on training for success. I had done a fair amount of independent training and self-coaching. During my sophomore year track season, I flourished while running with the boys' team under the coaching of Mr. Gould, who during cross-country season was the boys' head coach. Just a few months later when cross-country rolled around, I wanted to still run with the guys, since I was at least a minute in front of the second fastest female runner on my team. I felt it was only fair for me to run with people who could push me. After all, everyone else did. Moreover, during my sophomore year, my teammate Nora and I were often allowed to run with the boys, but since now it was only me, I seemed to be held back from this accommodation because singling me out "seemed elitist."

Given my personality and focused goal on becoming the best I could be, this new rule bothered me. It made me feel like I was being deprived of one of the most obvious tools to help me realize my dreams. This created conflict with Mr. Keene, who interpreted it as me "not being a team player." The truth is, had I been a more effective communicator, I could have shared my reasoning. I felt that in order to best help the team, I should be the fastest I could be. My thinking was that if I ran faster, I would pull the team along to quicker times, helping us achieve better scores in races.

For years I blamed myself entirely for being kicked off the team, but as my mom recalled the events as they actually happened, I realized that Mr. Keene and I both mishandled the situation. As a coach, Mr. Keene could be unclear in his motives, often not sharing why we were doing something the way we were doing it. Had I known this information, I might have been more

73

on-board with his plan and trusted his decisions. I became very invested in the physiology and science of training. I simply needed to know why we were doing certain workouts, or the reason he wanted me to run a certain slower pace with teammates on a given day.

A couple of weeks before I was dismissed from the team, we had traveled down by bus to North Carolina to run in The Great American Invitational. The trip was a blast, but during the race, in a mud pit on the golf course (there had been substantial rains the week before the race), my foot got sucked into deep mud. I struggled vigorously to pull it out, but a girl ran right over it in her racing spikes. Searing pain traveled from my foot up to my head. *OUCH*. During the race, adrenaline pumping, I knew that I had severely injured myself, but adrenaline masks pain and I had yet to realize the full extent of the damage. I finished the race with some limping, but kept a fairly aggressive pace. Upon completion, Mr. Gould had to carry me all the way back to our team's "camp" (where we kept our bags and hung out before our races). I was hardly able to walk, and within hours, my foot was roughly the size of a football. We iced it, but I was worried it was something worse.

My foot remained swollen the next day on the long return bus trip to Massachusetts. I took the day off from training and took round-the-clock Ibuprofen. The following day, my foot was much better. Swelling was localized just on top of my foot, and it barely hurt to walk. Because this was my first injury, I had no idea how to tell that this minor discomfort was something I needed to be concerned about and was indicative of more than the acute sprains or minor strains that I had previously encountered.

I managed to continue training. We figured that I sprained my foot, or perhaps suffered a bone bruise from getting stepped on in the mud pit. After a week or so, it became clear to me that my foot was not healing. But I continued to train. It did not seem to be getting worse – plus, with just a little Ibuprofen, I was fine. Mr. Keene held me back from running really hard in any of the dual meets so that I could rest up a little before the next big invitational. This was a relief for me, because when I would try to run fast on my own while the team was doing a workout and I was doing my own training, I would try to push my pace to test it, only to encounter worsening pain. After doing one workout at Amherst College, I knew my foot was in bad shape. I limped back to the high school with some slower friends, pretending I just wanted to chat with them, but really I was in too much pain to run back at my normal pace.

I did not want Mr. Keene to keep me from running, so I pretended the injury was not an issue. However, the day that I was kicked off the team, my foot was killing, even during school. I later found out that it was broken. It was the week of the Brown Invitational – one of the best races we ran every year because the course was pancake-flat with lots of competition to spur you on, so you were nearly guaranteed to set a huge personal record (PR). I could not walk around without trying to pawn some of my weight off onto the wall, radiators, or desks.

"We are going to do a workout over at Amherst College," Mr. Keene announced when I got to practice. *Uh-oh. I don't think I can run.* We started out on the warm-up toward the college campus. I winced in pain. Mr. Keene usually drove over to Amherst College to meet us after our warm-up. Halfway there, I decided to turn around and run back to school. I did not articulate clearly to my teammates the reason that I was doing this. Subsequently, when they reported that I had run back to school, I believe Mr. Keene thought that I blew off the workout, setting a very poor example that I was not going to do the hard work, and also that I could do whatever I wanted to do because I was the best.

This was not the case, and had he really thought about my personality, he should have known that I would not just bow out of a workout. I wanted to be fast; I loved working hard. But power struggles and conflicts over running with the boys' team during the previous weeks between us made him question my decision to walk back to school, and he thought I was using foot pain as an excuse to do my own thing.

I ended up limping almost all the way back to school, and I sat in the nearby graveyard for a while and cried. Yes, this sounds like clichéd teenage angst, but I liked the solace, and it was a bright, open graveyard rather than a typical eerie one portrayed in a creepy horror film. I knew my foot was broken and my season would be done. I didn't even see Mr. Keene when he got back, because my mom picked me up early for oboe lessons on Tuesdays. I told her about my foot, and she called the orthopedist to set up an appointment, using the leverage that I was a "very elite runner" and needed to be seen right away. We got an appointment for the next day during school, something my mom would rarely pull me from, particularly because it also meant her missing work – but I think she could tell by the look in my eyes that I needed her to give me this. "We'll see Dr. McBride tomorrow."

After Mom dropped me at my oboe lesson, she had to go back to the school to pick up my sister Emily. Mr. Keene approached her, furious that I had bailed on the workout, and told my mom that I was kicked off the team. According to my mom, he did not have anything substantive to say except that I was "not a team player" and was "no longer allowed on or near the team." I had to return my uniform and clean out my locker, and I was not to communicate with teammates. Mom, having just dealt with me sobbing in pain, had to get Emily home before picking me up from my oboe lesson, and so she did not have time to get sucked into a lengthy conversation with Mr. Keene. She was already displeased with him for allowing me to run, being so thin. She was somewhat relieved that all signs were pointing to the fact that I was going to be taking a break from running.

When Mom picked me up, she told me that I was kicked off the team. Mr. Keene had not even bothered to tell me directly. I burst into tears. Mom, being a woman of compassion and support, hugged me until I stopped crying. "It's okay, Am. You're going to get through this." I know that she hated seeing me in physical pain, and she understood that I was in tremendous emotional pain. Being a mental health professional, she grasped how depressed I was already and how critical running was to keeping my mood remaining just positive enough to save me from the depths of inescapable depression. I can only imagine how painful it is for a parent to see his or her child struggle so much with a devastating illness like anorexia. Yet at the same time, loving parents want the child to be happy and successful and enjoy her "stardom."

The next day I was subdued and withdrawn. During the school day, most of my teammates had not heard about my removal from the team. I avoided them as I was told to. At Dr. McBride's office, a simple x-ray showed that I had sustained a stress fracture in my third metatarsals. He informed us that although it was a stress fracture (a crack in the bone) rather than a complete fracture, the majority of stress fractures are not bad enough to show up on an x-ray and can only be identified by finer diagnostics, such as an MRI scan. My stress fracture must have existed for several weeks in order to be so clearly visible with crude imaging technology. That timing placed the injury back to exactly around the Great American Race. I had been running on a broken foot.

Dr. McBride said I needed to be non-weight bearing as much as possible and use crutches for walking. I could cross-train – in the pool would be optimal, followed by the bike after I could walk without pain. I would be re-evaluated in six weeks, with the prognosis that hopefully I could return to light jogging in six to eight weeks.

As expected, it was a very trying time for me. I hated pool running; it was excruciatingly boring. Simulating running while going nowhere in the water is the epitome of tedious exercise. Whereas I could not get enough when I ran outside, time inched by in the pool. Sometimes, if I was lucky, I would have company in the pool. After a few weeks, it seemed that it was forgotten that I was to have no interaction with teammates. Two of my favorite girls on the team would sometimes cross-train to give their bodies a break from the pounding endured during traditional running. I loved going to the pool with either or both of them, and since they were sisters, I enjoyed their back-and-forth bickering and teasing. They made me laugh, and conversations during the monotonous pool running helped pass the time.

Other times, my mom would drive me to pick up Colin, a friend that had been in the group of guys I ran with sophomore year, but who had since graduated and was attending UMass. He played Ultimate Frisbee on a club team and felt like he could stand to get some extra exercise. I don't know how, but Colin actually enjoyed pool running. It was fun for me because Colin's completely relaxed attitude toward the whole thing offered a welcome breath of fresh air. He would always take so long in the locker room that I would have already been in the pool for a good 12 to 15 minutes by the time he joined me. Because I was eagerly awaiting his appearance through the carwash noodle-like rubber curtain, I would be distracted and time would fly.

Once he finally rinsed off and was in the water, I would be almost halfway through a solid workout. Plus, just after he got in, he would often decide he wanted a floatation belt, hop out, and go try on the selection of belts. I'd watch him pick one, try it on, adjust it, then take it off and try another, as if that one would somehow be much more comfortable. Later, when I was back to training on the roads, Colin continued to be a entertaining training companion for random weekend runs – always stopping to "stretch" or constantly battling the perils of "ribsy" (the pain he named for a rib he had bruised in an Ultimate Frisbee game).

Although there were the rays of light in which I had company, I almost always trained by myself, which left me feeling completely detached. I only had a few friends left that had not graduated, and most of those were people I was told to avoid. The isolation resulted in harrowing depression. With each passing day, I felt increasingly forgotten, and more and more alone.

The first weekend after being kicked off the team, I traveled down to watch the Brown Invitational with my parents, even though I was instructed not to. I crutched out far away from the team and sat on a woodpile to cheer Emily and my former friends. One of my best friends from the previous year, Owen, who had graduated, was running for Brown University's team and kept me company.

It was the first race that I had ever needed to sit out that I wanted to be running. There had been dual meets where Mr. Keene had "rested" me, and perhaps I had run a workout of sorts instead, but I'd never missed a big invitational. Plus, it was one of my favorite courses – a wide, flat, wooded trail winding along the Atlantic Ocean. It was the best of both worlds – woods, which I had always loved, and fast running terrain. It was where I set my season PR for both my freshman and sophomore years. I had made it a season goal to run under 18 minutes. Brown's course was my best bet (I had run 18:03 at an early season race on another flat course at Hampshire College, setting the course record), but now that was not going to be attainable.

As a dedicated runner, it is very painful to watch other athletes run the race you feel born to dominate. Stuck on crutches, I felt physically removed from even the possibility of racing, and mentally my spirits had been eradicated, since I was no longer even part of the team.

I started to get better at cross-training. When I got over the initial mental setback of being kicked off the team and coming to terms with my first side-lining injury, I became just as obsessive about cross-training as I had been about running – perhaps even more. I was convinced that I needed to cross-train about twice as many minutes as I would have run, because running was a more physically demanding exercise. I started adding biking to the pool running. My goal was to get to the gym as quickly as possible after school, in order to maximize the number of minutes on my modalities before my mom would pick me up on her way home from work. While at first I took the school bus to the gym, one of my friends, Evan, later offered to drive me directly, since I was still on crutches. I saved about twenty minutes thanks to his door-to-door transportation – twenty minutes I could spend exercising.

Because there was not a way to quantify pool running other than elapsed time (whereas for running you can measure miles, pace you ran in a workout, or use other metrics), I became obsessed with accruing each minute. When Evan would chat with friends after school or dawdle leaving school, I would get irritable and edgy. I needed to get to the gym to start my workout. My single-minded focus on exercise was worse than it had ever been with running. I became irritable and cranky, and God forbid Mom came early, I'd be further aggravated. I wanted to train hard and train long. This obsession aligned with the anorexia: excessive exercise with a single-minded focus on training and burning calories.

Pool running is amazingly monotonous. Where I could listen to music while on the stationary bike, in the pool, it's just you and the wall. Pool running can only be executed properly in the deep end of the pool, so I would go in small, repetitive circles. The lifeguards gawked at me, and many swimmers asked me what I was doing. I hated being anybody's focus and I hated questions. The good days were when one of my friends, Brooke, was the lifeguard. I knew she wasn't staring and instead, she would engage in conversation with me. While we talked, I would bob around in small circles in front of her lifeguarding chair. The time went infinitely faster. Customers that I knew from Hastings also frequented my gym, since it was the primary fitness facility in Amherst, and they all felt perfectly comfortable asking me what I was doing and when I would be running again. In hindsight, I'm sure I was quite the spectacle: an emaciated girl "running" madly in the deep end of the pool (something that no one else ever did) for an hour at a time.

As the weeks went by, Mr. Keene felt remorse for what had happened. He tried reaching out to me, extending an olive branch, and asked me to rejoin the team just in time for the Western Massachusetts Championships. I wasn't having it. I was mad about what had happened, and the emotional suffering I went through when everything I loved was taken away from me. It was embarrassing when teammates would ask me why I was removed from the team and painful to lose my main group of friends, being asked to stay away. I had spiraled into a bad depression, focusing only on the gym and school. I wore my bathing suit under my clothes during school so that I could change as fast as possible, reducing my preparation time and increasing available time devoted to working out. I had slaved away hours in the pool over the weeks, fighting boredom and staying disciplined. It was going to take more than a little apology from Mr. Keene to entice me to join the team again. At this point, about six weeks had gone by, and I had missed most of the season. More importantly, I felt like a real outsider.

During the week of the Western Massachusetts Championships, I had my follow-up with the orthopedist, Dr. McBride. The new x-ray of my foot revealed a healed bone. I was cleared to run as long as I had no pain. Mr. Keene jumped in, hoping I would run the important race. I said no. I continued to cross-train, convinced it was too soon to run. *How could it be all better in six weeks?* The orthopedist had initially said six to eight weeks to heal, and my concern was that if I started back before it was done healing, it would break again.

After the race was over, Emily was upset that she had a bad race, and Mr. Keene was not impressed. Because I was not running and had dreamed of winning the Western Massachusetts Championships since the previous year, I was heartbroken. The injury had been a real blow to my ego, heart, and spirit. I was a shell of my former bubbly self. There is a poignant photo of Emily and me at the finish line. The photo shows us walking together away from the camera, arms around one another's backs, sharing in each other's pain, there for each other. The photo encapsulates our solidarity and the love we had for each other, even when our coach was upset with us and we were disappointed in ourselves. I look at that photo today and feel comforted in knowing that we always have each other, even when it feels like we have lost everything else that was important to us.

After nearly another week without running, my mom asked me why I was still cross-training and not out on the roads. "I'm not sure it's better yet; I want to wait." In my head I thought that I had pain, even though I did not – just a mild discomfort that the orthopedist said was totally normal and due to the healed bone getting accustomed to movement. Mom, understanding the psyche, knew I needed reassurance. She had me speak to Dr.

McBride again, who said I could run. "Why don't you try running, Am?" Mom suggested. I went for an easy mile, albeit tentatively, but my foot felt fine. Mr. Keene continued to urge me to rejoin the team and run in the State Championships, just a few days away. *I'm not ready for that. I haven't run in weeks!*

Over the course of the week, Dr. McBride's permission for me to run sank in a little more. I decided I would consider running in the State Championships, as long as my foot felt okay. Two days before the race, on a Thursday afternoon, my mom picked me up early from school and drove me two hours to Franklin Park in Boston, where the race was being held. She knew that I needed this. I wanted to see what the course was like. She waited while I completed the five-kilometer course, jogging at an easy pace along the well-marked path. I was discouraged that it did not feel as natural as running had always been. I felt like the rusted Tin Man from *The Wizard of Oz*, robotic in my motions and not fluid in my stride. However, much to my relief, I felt no pain. The course was relatively flat and wound through some woods, and had field sections. There were few hills, only one of which was substantial. I jogged back to the car as darkness fell around Boston. "Thanks Mom," I said, "I can do this." We drove all the way back to Amherst, with Mom allowing the light to be on in the car for me to study my for European History exam.

The day before the race, I rested my foot by pool running for an easy forty-five minutes. I write this sentence now and see the irony in it: "easy forty-five minutes." I would kill to have that discipline and level of fitness now. I sheepishly went to the pasta dinner that night, worried my teammates would not welcome me back. Everyone was thrilled to see me and treated me just as they always had. Later that night, I lay in bed, eyes wide open, worrying. *Will I make it through all three miles? Will I be able to run fast?* I had only jogged gently on Thursday, and I feared running at a race pace.

Saturday was the big day. It was a cold, rainy November morning, the kind where you just want to curl up in bed. But I was anxious to race. My teammates welcomed me on the bus with excited fanfare, presenting me with motivational notes and big hugs. I felt like a puppy separated from her litter, only to be rejoined with joyous litter-mate play.

When we arrived in Boston, I jogged most of the course with the team. Typically, we walked the first half and jogged the second half. I nervously jogged the second half with the slower few varsity runners, imagining myself trying to fly over this same ground just an hour later. "You can do it, Am," Emily offered. "You'll be great!"

We were freezing cold crowded behind the starting line. An icy drizzle fell around us. Girls from all teams began to get in their boxes (designated areas along the starting line) and do final race preparations. I had yet to run fast. Mr. Keene instructed me, "Try a few strides, Amber." On the first one, I ran barely faster than the warm-up pace, but then I did a few more progressively faster. *I can do this. I'm going to be just fine.* Our team huddled together. We sang our song. "And when we reach out to claim the gold, every man will know." I scanned the faces of all the girls on my team as I nervously whispered the words. Each face I looked at smiled back at me as our eyes met.

The starting line was quiet. I watched my warm breath dance like a cartoon ghost away from my mouth and drift down the field. We stood still, one leg in front of the other, bracing our bodies. "You'll see the flag come up, then hear the gun," boomed the starter through the megaphone. *Go get 'em, champ.*

The race went out fast. I got swallowed in the large funnel that formed as the long string of runners narrowed into a small path. *I can't stay here. I need to move up.* I started passing groups of girls, whole teams it seemed, as I moved toward the front. The path was mushy. Mud sprayed onto my singlet as girls in front of me kicked their feet up behind them. After about a mile, I passed my team's camp. Their cheers carried me. I passed everyone except the leader, Sara Powell from Oliver Ames. For the next two miles, I stayed strong. While I was not able to close the gap on Sara, I ran a courageous race and was thrilled with my second-place finish.

Our team re-grouped as our runners crossed the line. Mr. Keene jogged over to meet and congratulate us. He put his hands on my shoulders and looked me squarely in the eyes. "That was a gutsy race, kid." I knew he was proud. My friends surrounded me, hugging me and lifting me up. It was a close race, and we did not know how our team had fared. While we waited with baited breath for the results, parents offered their input. "I counted Amherst with the win. Oliver Ames second." "I don't know, I think Attleboro was right up there."

The moment we received the news that we won the State Title, there was palpable excitement and a visible glow of pride across our faces. It is a moment I will never forget. On the cooldown jog around the course, I was nothing but smiles. My foot felt fine and I leapt and played in my normal, carefree manner along the path with my friends.

26.
Therapy, Amber

SHORTLY AFTER THE END of the cross-country season during my junior year of high school, I started seeing a local psychiatrist once a week. I'm not exactly sure why we waited so long for me to see a mental health professional. To this day, that boggles my mind. Perhaps because both of my parents work in the mental health field, they knew more about what therapy could or couldn't offer me and figured it was not a good fit at the time. If this was the case, to their credit, they were right: I was not ready.

The appointment time was split equally between my mom and I each seeing the psychiatrist separately, and then together. I couldn't stand the psychiatrist. She said my name at the beginning and end of every statement or question, which got under my skin. "Amber, can you tell me how that makes you feel, Amber?" Or, "Amber, I'd like you to explain to me why it is important to you to continue running, Amber." One time, she came into Hastings while I was working, and due to patient-doctor confidentiality, politely pretended she didn't know me, but winked when I rang up her purchases: a birthday card with an elephant in a party hat and a roll of LifeSavers.

The psychiatrist prescribed me Celexa, an antidepressant. Maybe the medication contributed to my eventual recovery, but it is hard to say since I never really felt its effects, even as she increased my dosage. Anyway, the therapy didn't accomplish very much except to stir up more animosity between me and my mother. However, there was one night when we walked back down the car, neither of us muttering a word to one another. Finally, Mom broke the ice. "What's the matter, Am?" "Nothing. I just hate how she keeps saying my name." We drove down through the center of town in silence. After a minute or two, Mom said, "She's an annoying woman in general, isn't she?" My mom looked at me, and we both smiled.

Neither the Celexa nor the therapy spurred me to eat, improved my body image, or got me to be less obsessive about running. As the dosage was doubled, I just felt increasingly numb to all emotions. Running well had a smaller impact on making me feel good. Depression felt more inevitable but bothered me less. I had a harder time staying motivated with homework, but I was lucky that I was intelligent and could skate by relatively easily and still earn solid grades.

27.
"May I Sketch Your Face?"

MOST OF THE TIME, my eating disorder went completely unmentioned. My peers did not confront me about it, and people did not talk about it, at least to my face. This was probably due to a few factors. First and foremost, I was very young when the anorexia developed. There weren't very many ten-year-olds in the small town of Amherst who knew what anorexia was or what signs and symptoms to look for. I mention Amherst specifically because after living in New York City for the past four years, I think city children might recognize it more easily. But perhaps all I am really noticing is the changing of times, and that kids in 2013 are more aware of eating disorders than kids were in 1996.

In elementary school, I was always the smallest in the class. I think this caused friends who knew me well through the early years of the disease to assume I was just still tiny Amber. Most probably did not suspect I had an issue. I had always looked like the little sister of my peers. In the early years of my disease, I wasn't losing any noticeable weight – I just wasn't gaining anything, while everyone else was. "Amber's a late bloomer...always has been" everyone said, including my family.

However, in high school, when my body was clearly skeletal rather than just petite, my anorexia was harder to overlook. One afternoon after work, I went running through the University of Massachusetts campus with James. When we were about to head down Eastman Lane for the return trip, a woman yelled out of her car window, "GET SOME HELP! You're anorexic!" I don't know if James didn't hear, didn't care, or didn't know she was yelling about me, but he just ignored the comment and launched into a story about some action movie. I tuned him out because my mind was filled with anger and hurt, as thoughts about the jeer raced through my inner dialogue.

Another time I was working at Hastings and a hefty guy wearing suspenders leaned across the counter, into earshot of my coworker and me. "You look like you just got out of a concentration camp." My face flushed with embarrassment, but I couldn't think of anything to say. Thankfully, my coworker brushed it off and didn't make a big deal of the situation. It wasn't the first time I had heard a comment like that one. When I was volunteering at the Soup Kitchen, a homeless man offered to sketch my face. "That's okay," I said. (I hated people staring at me.) He did anyway. "Here. You look like Anne Frank, so I was intrigued." He handed me a napkin with a pretty accurate pencil rendition of my wan, concave face.

Due to the nature of the disease, anorexia is an extremely difficult subject to broach. Whether the individual displaying signs of an eating disorder is related to you, or is a friend, teammate, peer, one of your athletes, or a neighbor, the conversation is never an easy one. One of the defining characteristics of the disease is denial about weight being a problem, denial about calories eaten or expended, and defensiveness. I was a perfect textbook example of this aspect of the disease. One friend made a joking comment when we were in the seventh grade about how I "ate like someone with anorexia." I got so mad at her that we didn't speak for a week (which, in the lives of seventh grade girls, is a long time!). In hindsight, I can see it was her attempt to reach out to me about my illness.

When I finally did start eating again, I received one of my most upsetting comments. *Pasta Y Basta*, a local Italian place, had great rosemary and olive oil focaccia. You could buy four pieces, heated up and wrapped in tinfoil, for a dollar. It became one of my favorite pre-work snacks while I was recovering. One time when I was checking out, the guy ringing me up said, "I hope you eat more than this. You look disgusting." Needless to say, I felt utterly disgusting eating all four pieces of bread.

28.
"You are Ten Years Old"

ONE OF MY LEAST favorite appointments was the endocrinologist down at Baystate, the hospital in Springfield, MA. First of all, I hated going because it was a pretty lengthy drive at 45 or 50 minutes, which usually meant that I would miss practice. Secondly, the tall, burly Eastern European male nurse was rough with measuring my height and weight – pushing me against the wall, speaking in an accent I couldn't understand. I had no idea what he was asking me to do.

My pediatrician referred me to the endocrinologist due to a "lack of physical evidence that I had begun puberty." I was closing in on seventeen years old, and according to the Tanner Stages (a scale used to evaluate pubertal development through primary and secondary sex characteristics), I was still developmentally about that of a 10-year-old, or a Tanner Stage between 1 and 2.

The endocrinologist ran specialized lab work, which showed what was expected – abnormally low levels of sex hormones. Eventually the medical team working with my family decided the solution was the obvious one – I needed to gain body fat.

During appointments, the endocrinologist would critique my naked body, which was incredibly embarrassing because he did so in front of my mom. You pretty much lose all your dignity when a doctor is trying to teach your mom about your lack of pubic hair by comparing parts of your body to medical photos of "normal development." I could drive a stick shift, but I couldn't grow pubic hair.

29.
Ariel Childs

ARIEL CHILDS WAS ONE of my good friends during my adolescence. Although she lived in my neighborhood, we only became friends in seventh grade, because she had attended a different elementary school. We had a few things in common: we were both standout athletes (she was a gymnast), we both had older sisters that we loved, and we struggled to find happiness despite outsiders' impressions that we had all of our ducks in a row. "Ari" was in many of my classes in seventh grade, and we both started learning Chinese.

I liked talking to Ari about the pressures of excelling in our sports. We both would get nervous for competitions, not wanting to let our fans or ourselves down. We both equally mourned the loss of our older sisters when they graduated and left us with sister-sized holes in our hearts. We talked about our parents and how sometimes the things they did felt so out of line. Ari and I helped one another with homework assignments, practiced Chinese, and passed dozens of motivational, supportive notes and letters back and forth over the years. We made mix CDs, found inspirational quotes appropriate for each other, and talked online in the evenings. Ari was a huge supporter of my highs and a comforting shoulder to hold me during my lows. We weren't really friends that hung out much after school, but our relationship was very important nonetheless.

30.
The Armory

I DIDN'T RUN INDOOR track my freshman year because my school did not have a program yet. It started to form loosely toward the middle of that winter, but it was not really a coached, established program, so my parents did not want me to do it. "You need a break from competing." I was fine with that, because I had been training on my own after school most days and was enjoying it. In many ways, I was probably training harder than I would have with the team – regularly pushing my pace for a sixty-minute run. I enjoyed the solitude as well as being able to run whatever I felt like – not just what I was told. When I was tired, I ran less. When I felt strong, I pushed harder. Sometimes I would start out with teammates and then branch off and do my own thing, but generally, I hit the pavement alone.

Sophomore year, my parents were concerned about my weight at the close of the cross-country season. Because my weight was too low, they did not permit me to start indoor track when the season officially began. I had developed strong friendships with some of the runners on the boys' team during that cross-country season, and I missed running with them. "When are you joining indoor, Am?" I worried that if I didn't run with them, I would not be pushed enough. After all, their race times were much faster than mine. I worked on convincing my parents to allow me to run indoor track, and after the New Year, they agreed.

At the season's close, I ran the two-mile at Indoor Nationals at the Armory in New York City. It was fun to be in the "big city," and I remember being terrified that I was going to get lost on my warm-up. As a result, I ran around and around a small playground. I did fine in the race, nothing spectacular, ending in sixteenth place. However, the following year is what I vividly remember. My junior year, I wanted to run the same Indoor Nationals at the Armory. This time, I was interested in the 5,000m, which was on a Friday night, and the two-mile, which was on Sunday afternoon. The trick would be to convince my mom to take me there to run, since no one else on the team had qualified.

My mom could see from the sparkle in my eye that this was a race that I really wanted to do. "Do you have to do both?" she asked. We decided I would register for both events, and then after Friday's 5,000m, she and I would evaluate if we were up for making the trip again on Sunday. We could not afford to stay in New York for three days, so we would have to drive down and back both days. Additionally, I still worked the early Sunday morning shift - a shift that was extremely difficult to get a substitute for because it required special knowledge of opening procedures that only our boss knew how to do. I arranged that if I was going to run Sunday's two-mile, I would get there at 5:30 and do the opening procedures with James, and then get relieved at 8:00 a.m. when it was business as usual, so anyone on the staff could fill in for me.

On Friday afternoon, my mom drove my sister Ashleigh and I down to the Armory Track and Field Center in Manhattan. Ashleigh opted to come down and cheer for me, which I was thrilled about. I could use all the support I could get. The drive down felt long. Because I was hydrating for the race, I had to pee so badly as we entered the outskirts of the Bronx. There were no bathrooms in sight. Finally, Mom pulled over at a playground that had a restroom. I desperately jumped out of the car with Ashleigh. The bathroom was locked. "Just go behind it, Amber." With cars driving by and locals walking the sidewalks, I peed for a solid minute behind the restroom shed.

At the Indoor Nationals race, you are given a special singlet to wear that has the name of your state on it. We picked up my singlet and race registration. I warmed up for the 5,000m at the playground I remembered from the year before. As I was stretching inside with Mom, another small girl was being stretched by her father. "She's a real champion," he said, "and she's only twelve." Her name was Briana Jackucewicz, and I decided I *had* to beat her. I think my mom was on the same wavelength. "You put her in her place, champ. She's got nothing on you." Then she tried to stretch my legs too. "It's 25 laps, Mom," I said. "That's so many!" "Just take them one at a time." I had never run five kilometers on a track – let alone an indoor track, which is half the size of an outdoor. For a girl with ADHD, 25 laps sounds like an eternity.

We lined up on the steep-banked track. The indoor stadium was stuffy and loud. The gun went off. The rhythm of feet running over the raised wooden track thumped along: *bam bam bam bam*. I felt sucked into a jet stream of fast running. I counted down laps each time I passed the start. Energetic cheering filling the entire arena. I ran 17:19.27, good for second place! It was my first 5,000m under 18 minutes. I beat Briana, who finished in fifth. I was thrilled. It was an incredible feeling to stand on the podium, bowing my head to receive my medal. *Second in the nation?! I'm getting good.*

Ashleigh came with me on my cool-down, and we ventured a little further around Washington Heights. "You should do the two-mile." I knew she was right. We ran past bodegas, little flower stands, and an automobile shop. We talked about where I might want to go to college, and how she liked school now that she had transferred to Kenyon from Smith. It was one of my favorite runs I ever did with Ashleigh, even though it was just an extended cool-down – maybe twenty minutes at most. I truly felt her support and her admiration of my hard work and success. Even though I was her younger sister, I could sense her respect.

I did in fact return Sunday morning to run the two-mile, after begging a coworker to take the second half of my shift. The 5,000m had not taken too much out of me, although I was a little sore. I rolled out of bed extra early that morning to pack my race bag and drive to work at 5:20 a.m. My mom arrived at 8:00 a.m. with my favorite bagels (yes, I ate two), but my coworker was nowhere in sight. Watching the minutes tick by on the clock, I worried we would not make it in time. Twenty minutes later, my substitute strolled in and mom gunned it for the city.

Ashleigh had returned to school, so it was just my mom and me. I ran the two-mile pretty well, getting 4th place in a solid 10:56, which was my fastest time indoor to date. On my cool-down, I ran the same loop I had done with Ashleigh, but this time, cloaked in loneliness, longing for her companionship. I talked to her in my head as I listened to the Spanish spoken throughout the neighborhood, the honks of cars, and the screeching bus brakes. As the sun was setting, I arrived back at the Armory, met up with my mom, and we headed back to Amherst for the start of the outdoor track season.

31.
One Thousand Paper Cranes

ONE SUNDAY AFTER WORK in April of my junior year, I pulled into the parking lot at my high school to go for a long run. My cell phone rang. It was my track coach, Chris Gould. He was also a social studies teacher at our high school and had been a part of my running career since the eighth grade. In many ways, Mr. Gould was as much (if not more) of a father to me than my own. He rarely called me, but I figured it might be about Penn Relays, which were just a few weeks away.

"Hey Amber, Chris Gould."

"Hi, Mr. Gould."

He went on to tell me that he had been having some abdominal pain that felt like he had a bad side stitch, or perhaps appendicitis. It flared up after a workout with the track team when he was pushing hard with the fastest guys. He figured he had pulled a muscle, but a few days later when the pain had not abated, he went to see his doctor. Tests revealed he had testicular cancer. I cannot imagine the feeling he or his family members experienced when they learned of this. All I know is that it must have been even worse than how I felt—my heart fell into my lap. *Cancer?! He's the healthiest guy I know.*

We talked for a few more minutes, but I was barely aware when our conversation had ended. My mind was racing and I couldn't listen. I know that he said he was going to be taking time off from coaching and was not going to be able to make it to Penn Relays. None of that mattered to me. I was just so worried that he was sick. After he asked me not to mention it to people, I snapped out of my daze. "Wait. Stop. Are you going to be okay?" "Yeah. I'm going to be okay." He said he had to go, and I sat in silence in my car, my phone still up to my ear. I held it there unconsciously for a few minutes, as if hoping he would call back and change the diagnosis.

A guy I knew from the soccer team drove by honking and waving. I dropped my phone and realized I was sitting in a numb stillness. It was hard to swallow. I was scared for Mr. Gould, scared for his wife, and scared for his daughters. *He doesn't deserve this.* Mr. Gould was one of the kindest hearts I had ever known. He knew how to be fair, yet tough, but he also had a heart of gold, the generosity of an angel, and an understanding that was unparalleled in other adults in my life, including my own father. He knew how to make me believe in myself, make me value myself, and he reminded me without explicitly saying so that I was important. With the self-esteem of a doormat that's been thrown away, I desperately needed an adult mentor in my life to help pull me up.

Even though I hit fast times, had my name revered in the paper several times per week, and was congratulated constantly by all walks of life in our student body, I hated myself. I felt unloved, unworthy of love and kindness, and like an outcast. Particularly in the wake of the loss of my friends to colleges during my junior year, the stress of feeling like my mom hated me for being anorexic, and other family issues, I relied heavily on his support.

Eventually I got out of my car. I didn't even consider how long I had been sitting there, or the fact that my mom calculated the time I should be home after a post-work run. I was definitely going to be late, which usually meant I had run too much and was in for a serious scolding and punishment. None of this crossed my mind. I didn't even start my watch, as I always did; I just started running. I remember exactly the run I did and the instant I burst into tears, right at the entrance to Amherst College. It is actually physically difficult to start crying while you are running. I'm guessing it has something to do with endorphins. But my heart was so heavy that the pressure had to be relieved in an explosion of tears.

I kept going. I covered most of our "usual" routes from the school – going the full route one way, then passing the school and doing a full route in the other direction. What must have been thirteen miles later, eyes bloodshot, blistering headache, and a heavy lump in my throat, I ran back to the parking lot. I was in such a speeding daze, I literally crashed into my car with my outstretched hands slamming onto the hood.

Without stretching, taking another step, or even allowing my heaving breath to calm, I got back in the car, my phone beeping every two minutes to alert me to the voicemails from my mom. The six-minute car ride home was a dull blur. Sheer muscle memory controlled my car. *Push down on the clutch. Stop at red. Go at green.* I rocketed into the driveway as I always did and went inside, still sweating.

"Where were you?!" Mom said, exasperated. I sat on the footstool in front of our dog's food bowl. I didn't answer. "Amber, what's going on?"

"Mr. Gould has cancer." I stood up and turned to walk upstairs, knowing she was furious at me for being so late, not calling, and probably running a zillion miles. But she walked over and touched my arm, pulling me in just in time before I crumbled into tears.

I honored my promise to not tell anyone on the team, but word of Mr. Gould's illness still managed to spread quickly. Although no one verbalized his or her concern, it was clear that the mood on the track team was heavy. I started doing my own thing every day and ditching the team. Without our distance coach, the sprints and jumps coach gave us workouts, but the team was so big that I escaped unnoticed to fend for myself. I would allow Mr. Gould's spirit to guide me while he wasn't there. A few weeks later, he was emailing us training schedules anyway.

Just a few weeks after my coach informed me of his illness, I returned to Penn Relays to run the same race (3,000m) that I ran the previous year, when I took the trip with him and the 4x800 relay team. This time, however, I came armed with much faster times heading into the race and a less rushed pre-race preparation. I'd traveled with my parents rather than Mr. Gould, who was working on battling his disease. My parents and I took a trip down to Washington D.C. prior to the race to tour Georgetown University (a prospective school) and enjoy the city for a few days. When I was in elementary school, there was a four- or five-year span where the family would routinely spend April vacation in Washington D.C. to desperately greet spring after a long New England winter, a little sooner than it would hit Massachusetts. After about a six-year hiatus, my parents, John (our new puppy), and I returned in April 2003.

I was not wild about Georgetown. As much as I always liked Washington D.C., the thought of moving to a city seemed like a grave mismatch for the rustic girl that I was at the time. (Strangely enough, I have lived in New York City – the most populous city in the country – for the past five years). In retrospect, I believe that I was having trouble focusing on the college visit because my mind was set on the impending Penn Relays. My goal was to break the ten-minute mark in the 3,000m, which seemed completely realistic, given that I ran 10:12.57 the year before when I was much less fit. My two-mile times (slightly longer than 200m further than the 3,000 race distance) were indicative that I should be able to run under ten. I also wanted to place in the top three and get a medal.

I remember looking up in the stands where Mr. Gould and my 4x800 teammates had cheered the year before. Unfamiliar faces filled their seats. I said a prayer for Mr. Gould's health. *In the name of the Father, the Son, and the Holy Spirit: Dear God, please, please, please give Mr. Gould the strength to beat the cancer. Please God, I don't ask you for much. I need him; the world needs him. I miss him. Please God, please give him his health back. Thank you. Amen.*

The race did not go well. All twenty-four qualifiers ran in one heat, which is a lot for such a competitive event. Crowding can lead to slower races because you cannot get a good position, or you get stuck on an inside lane, sandwiched in a group of girls you want to pass, unable to break free. Particularly for my conservative start style, crowded track races are not conducive for a top finish position. Penn Relays were no different.

For the first mile, I was stuck on the inside lane of the track in a pack of racers. I could not get out of the group. While the pace was not significantly slower than I wanted to be going, every second really counts on each lap when you are going for a specific time. More importantly, the stress of perceiving my position to be poor and recognizing that I was not running well, was exhausting. I would struggle to try to surge out of the pack, only to get sucked back in. The constant pace-changing and jostling from taller, bigger girls wore on me. In the final few laps, I was frustrated and tired. I ended in fourteenth place in a time of 10:20 – a very poor performance for me, particularly given my goals, previous races that season, and last year's breakout race at Penn Relays.

I told my mom that I did not want to talk about the race and went on a vigorous, lengthy cool-down through the campus, as if to beat myself up for bombing my race. The long drive home was quiet. My parents understood how disappointed I was, which meant that they knew to leave me be in my own headspace. I thought about how I needed to rectify my defeat and come back strong for the remainder of the track season. I had a big goal – to win the State Championships two-mile event. I did not want another "ride of shame" home.

During the time of his illness, I thought about Mr. Gould constantly – probably more than was healthy, but I have always tended toward obsession, and his health became one of mine. I would go over with cookies or strawberries for the family when I could and left them on the porch, not wanting to bother him. I got help from other students and athletes to make 1,000 paper cranes, after remembering a childhood book I read in which a Japanese girl made 1,000 paper cranes to heal her friend of cancer. I strung long chains of cranes from dowels, creating curtains of many colored paper birds, and delivered them to his house. Thankfully, Mr. Gould ended up beating the cancer into remission and is still healthy today.

32.
Nine Seconds

THE PREVIOUS YEAR, I had won the Western Massachusetts Championship in my goal-shattering 10:48, and I went on that season to place fourth in the State Championships in a slower time. My junior year, I was gunning for the win. A few months prior, I won the Indoor State Championships, but competition was stiffer outdoors so I was not as confident. The plan was to cruise through the win in the Western Mass race, resting up for the next week at States, where I would have my biggest competition – Sara Powell, the girl that beat me during the State cross-country championships. At this point, we were friendly from Penn Relays and a handful of other races. She was a senior, and I knew she really wanted the win. She had posted roughly the same two-mile times as me, but was significantly faster than me at shorter events.

The race came on a windy day in the small Eastern Massachusetts town of Norwell. On my warm-up, I ran past picnic areas and felt nervous. The track did not seem to be in the best condition. It had divots and needed patch work. More concerning, because I was such a light, wispy runner, I did not usually run well in the wind.

When the gun went off, I was ready. The race started exactly as I predicted. A few other highly talented girls took the early lead, and I remained within striking distance from them. I was hitting my planned splits. Then Sara took the lead. She started gaining distance on the rest of us, and I knew I needed to go after her right then if I was to stand a chance at the title, especially because I knew she had a faster kick (final sprint) than me.

During the fifth lap, I caught up. I took the lead. Sara reclaimed it. It seemed to be a dead heat. With one lap to go, the bell rang. She was leading. I needed to pass her. I started sprinting. My little legs were going as fast as I could make them go. She followed. *Did I start kicking too early? I still have 200m to go. Sara is going to leave me in the dust!* But something happened: I just kept kicking. I wanted the win with every step. The final 100m, as my form broke down from fatigue and my arms flailed a bit, I crossed the line nine seconds before her: a thrilling 10:45.15 to her 10:54.80. It was as if she had given up in the last straightaway, knowing the race was mine.

The following week, I went on to win the New England Championships two-mile race. I felt untouchable. All I had left was the Junior USA Track & Field National Championships in Palo Alto, where I was going to run the 5,000m.

33.
USATF Championships and Meeting Dena

IN JUNE OF 2003, I had just finished up my junior year and had qualified for the USA Track & Field Junior Nationals in Palo Alto, California. I had run Junior Olympic races before, but some of those had low barriers of entry (easier qualifying times) with more rounds to the Nationals as a result. This was a much bigger deal, because it was a larger age group (15-21 years old) as opposed to the two-year age categories of the Junior Olympics. Plus, freshmen in college with more competitive race experience under their belts were eligible to compete. Being such a prestigious race, the Junior Nationals drew some of the toughest competition – young hopefuls like me looking for a chance to represent the United States by qualifying for the Pan-American Games in Barbados. Plus, it was a perfect opportunity to tour Stanford University – my dream school.

With just a little persuasion, my mom agreed to travel to California for the race and campus visit. She was extremely supportive of me reaching my goals and knew for quite some time that I had been interested in Stanford. I had even set up a meeting with head coach Dena Evans.

Looking back, and even at the time, one of my favorite aspects of running fast was that it enabled me to have an excuse to travel. Growing up, we did very little traveling outside of New England. We were a rougher-the-better type of family – we backpacked on the Long Trail, or went on biking vacations or camping. There was the infamous time we spent eight days on a farm in Vermont and helped out with farm chores. It wasn't like we even splurged when we were on such adventures. We always ate from the communal teal lunch bag – hummus, pitas, Fig Newtons, and bruised pieces of fruit. When we went to summer camp, they were always rustic Girl Scout camps with latrines, unidentifiable food, and no-frills amenities. Don't get me wrong, I definitely enjoyed all of our trips. But they were exactly that – trips, not vacations.

When I became a competitive runner, I traveled to places where we stayed in hotels, I took airplane rides, and we went to my first Olive Garden. The experience was so novel and exciting to me that I wrote all about what everyone ordered, what our party's perceptions of the food was, and drew sketches of the breadsticks in my journal. These were exciting perks for me, but nothing beat all the alone time I got with my mom. Being the youngest of three girls with numerous extracurricular activities and having busy, working parents, I felt like I rarely got individual time with just one parent.

Championship races were different. Mom and I would go together, and for those few days, I felt like I was her world. We laughed together, avoided people we didn't feel like talking to, and explored the cities and towns by foot. Mom wasn't just good at the trip stuff – she was great with the running. She would help me size up the competition as we walked around the hotel or race course. She helped me make sure I had everything packed up in my race bag, ensuring that I would have my number and racing spikes when I stepped up to the starting line.

Mom was always up for walking the course with me and didn't mind if I bent her ear about what my strategy was going to be. During races, I could hear her voice above all others, and she would tell me exactly the things I told her I wanted to hear. Sometimes it was just to cheer me on. Others, she'd yell out a motivational phrase I had pre-selected, or how many meters behind me the next girl was. Because I yakked her ear off before the race, Mom knew the splits that I was trying to hit, and the names and uniform colors of all my rivals. I always got very nervous before races. Confidence was replaced by self-deprecation, feelings of fatigue and inadequacy, and anxiety. Mom knew the drill. She knew how to calm me down and what to say to get me positive and focused.

Mom was always willing to go wherever the race was. One time, she drove me and two friends five hours up to Maine for an all-day Junior Olympics track race and then back, another six or seven hours in heavy traffic. We went to Spartanburg, SC, all over New England and New York, Philadelphia, Sacramento, San Francisco, and other places. On one of the trips to California, we ventured to the Jelly Belly Jelly Bean Factory. Even in my most severe anorexic days, I've always had a sweet tooth, and you could find me eating candy.

I loved Jelly Bellies and was even part of their "Taste Testers Club," beginning around seventh grade. As a member of the club, I received a monthly package of new flavors of beans to sample and rate. I would spend a few hours choosing my ratings and drafting my comments on separate sheets of scrap paper before committing them to the official comment cards, knowing that they would be taken seriously once at the company. I received a pin and a t-shirt and felt like I was an official member of the company. At the time, I didn't realize there were probably thousands upon thousands of other tasters around the country.

Mom and I took the drive an hour or so to the factory from the race location on one of the afternoons between events. In the car, we always listened mixes I burned at home prior to the trip. She was cool about music. She liked anything I played and never complained.

It has only recently become clear to me that the expectations I have of things prior to experiencing them are much loftier than most other people's, and way off the mark of the actual event. For instance, my husband and I enjoy watching shows on the Food Network channel. When I saw that Giada De Laurentis was going to be at a book signing at the local Williams Sonoma, I thought that meant that Ben and I would go to the store, and she would meet us there with hopeful anticipation. Upon our warm reception, Giada would walk around privately with us, recommending products, sharing stories about her husband and daughter, and asking eagerly to see pictures of my dog, which I would show her on my phone. After an hour or so, she would ask if we would like to go to the Whole Foods Market downstairs for lunch. Apparently, it's just a line of people waiting to get a quick signature in her latest book you are expected to buy. Who knew?

Well, when I was younger, these grandiose visions of what was to come were often even further from reality that my current naivety. The Jelly Belly Jelly Bean Factory was no exception. I envisioned being greeted by Mr. Jelly Belly himself, offering a tray of beans to get me started. As we talked about how the traffic had been, we would enter the factory – which, in my mind, looked like a mini amusement park. I would be handed a lab coat with my name embroidered on the lapel and shown where to go. There, I would be mixing concoctions to design my own bean flavors and advise others who may need some inspiration. Then, operating all the machinery on my own, under the guidance of Mr. Bean, I would create as many bags of beans as I wanted. *Mom will make hot pepper on pita and I'll make Samoa Girl Scout Cookie.* After making our jelly beans, we would help box the beans, and I would get to drag my arms though barrels of the brightly colored candies.

In actuality, we weren't given any special recognition and were lumped in with dozens of Jelly Belly fans (likely members of the Taste Tester's Club) on a crowded, hot tour, with a guide whose accent I could not understand. Her only words I kept recognizing were "conveylor belt," which I understood meant the conveyor belt on the other side of the Plexiglas window that kept us out of the factory. At the end of the tour was a gift shop where Jelly Belly jelly beans cost even more than they did at our local supermarket back home. We left with one little bag, no free samples, and another dashed silent dream.

The meeting I had scheduled with the Stanford women's head coach, Dena Evans, during the trip to the USATF Junior Nationals was also not at all what I expected. I loved the California weather, and we toured the Stanford campus and it was a paradise of palm trees, vibrant buildings, and beautiful flowers. However, as I sat in Coach Evans' office for an interview, it became clear that she was the first coach that was not particularly eager for me to run on her team, although she did not explicitly articulate why. There was something about her mannerisms and the fact that she did not seem to be nearly as overzealous to recruit me as the dozens of other coaches that I had spoken to at other prospective schools. Most other "interviews" felt like the coach was trying to sell their school and program to me, some nearly down on their knees begging. Dena questioned me; she seemed to want me to sell myself. It was strangely unsettling.

The 5,000m race was at 9:00 p.m. local time, which, for my jet-lagged body, translated to midnight. I remember being so tired beforehand that I "wanted to fold." Mom knew exactly what to say to me to get me out of my grumbling and instead start warming up. Thankfully, I pulled out of my funk with her motivation and stepped on the line, knowing exactly where she would be to give me more words of encouragement on the track. To this day, the crystal-clear memory of Mom cheering me on for the 12.5 laps is emblazoned in my brain. I can picture exactly where she stood on the track and the fact that every time I was on the opposite side of the track, I thought to myself, *just halfway around and then I'll be back to Mom.*

The race was fantastic. I ran 17:07 and loved every minute of it. I earned All-American honors, the highest award in competitive running. We filled out the necessary paperwork for Barbados because there was a chance I would be selected for the team, since I was an alternate. Somehow I got it in my head that I would be going to Barbados with Team USA.

34.
The Seeds are Planted

INDEED, A FEW WEEKS later, when I was working one night, I got the call that I was moved up and selected to represent Team USA in Barbados, if I so chose. *If I so choose?! Of course!* There are many things about the trip to Barbados that I remember: the flight to Miami where the whole team met up, the fact that I was the second youngest (and by far the tiniest) of the group, the huge duffle bag of Team USA gear we received, the oppressing heat of running there, the fact that the women's spandex shorts in extra-small were incredibly baggy on my spindly thighs, my roommate Laura Zeigle pulling out a Bible on the bus, and the guy who became my "surrogate dad" for the trip, Dave Templin. Above all, I remember that that trip was the breaking point in my anorexia – the point that I got things turning back toward health and away from the disease.

The month before, my mindset began changing. The little angel in my head (who I had considered to be a detrimental devil during the depths of my anorexia) was saying, "Come on, Am, let's start to eat. Let's kick this thing." I remember sitting at the family computer in our living room, excited to open up my email account. Emails from coaches trying to set up visits with me had been flooding my inbox for weeks. This particular morning, I received an email from Dena, the coach at Stanford. It confirmed the sense that I perceived during our meeting, which indicated that my interest in running for Stanford was not reciprocated.

The email said that it was wonderful to meet me and she liked me a lot. She said that I seemed like a great academic fit for Stanford and she would be interested in the opportunity to coach me, but had concerns about my weight. While she did not directly call me out on having an eating disorder, Dena said she had "experience with other female athletes will extremely low body fat," and since they were so injury-prone, she was "concerned that the rigor of the training would be too much for my body." It was a wakeup call. It was the first time any of the dozens of coaches that had recruited me had ever pointed out the obvious – I was skeletally thin – or mentioned anything about eating disorders.

In hindsight, it just seemed to be a topic coaches totally ignored, either because they did not want to insinuate that any prospective athlete had an issue because it is a uncomfortable to discuss, or because they did not care because they knew that some of the fastest female runners *did* have eating disorders. At the time, I figured these coaches saw me as I saw myself – an elite runner with an elite runner's body. *Finally. A life where people aren't hounding me to eat the way my high school coaches and parents do. These coaches know I am perfect.*

Dena was the first to prove that thought process wrong, and it was particularly impactful because Stanford had been my top choice as a prospective student for quite some time. I would like to say that the concerns Dena articulated in her email immediately reached me and I started eating – but eating disorders, particularly long-term ones (and mine had been going on for almost seven years at that point) are very deeply rooted. However, Dena's email was a voice that I couldn't get out of my head, even if it did not immediately turn things around. Truthfully, a couple of times in the next few weeks before the trip to Barbados, when I encountered the intense hunger I was accustomed to ignoring, I instead asked myself, "Is it okay if I eat this apple or this extra bit of veggie burger?" Then I would think, *yes, just a little might be okay. I don't want Dena to think I am too anorexic to run for Stanford.* These moments were few and far between, but they were the first of this type of internal dialogue, and at least had planted the seed that I might not be living a sustainable, champion-like lifestyle.

35.
Apple Hill

I STARTED PLAYING OBOE in fifth grade, and I usually went to a music camp for at least a few weeks during the summer shortly thereafter. My parents strongly urged me to pursue music with an equal amount of time and passion as I devoted to running. While I loved this arrangement when I was younger, as I grew to be highly competitive and obsessed with running in high school, I felt that the two rehearsals and one lesson per week detracted from the time I had for running, as well as the energy I needed to recover from practice. Often with races, I would have to rush back so I could get to a lesson. I hated that.

In the couple of weeks between the USATF Junior Nationals at Stanford and the Junior Pan American Games in Barbados, I went to music camp in New Hampshire. It was my second consecutive year going to Apple Hill Chamber Music Camp. Unlike the music camps I had attended when I was younger, Apple Hill was geared towards adults, and I was one of just a handful of teenagers that attended. The camp provided very little supervision. It was just a place filled with musicians who had daily organized lessons and chamber music groups. Campers spent the rest of their days as they pleased. Despite the hilly terrain, I did a fair amount of running, as might be imagined. I also read James Baldwin's *Another Country*, practiced musical arrangements, made oboe reeds, and complained on the phone to my family about one of my cabin-mates, Katy, who was bulimic.

Although I was also battling an eating disorder, I was in the initial stages of contemplating life without the disease. I was at a particularly vulnerable stage in that transition: I was still restricting all of my food and living like an anorexic person, but my brain was shifting – wondering what my life would be like if I stopped. Katy's bulimia was not only disgusting to me (because she would literally eat in our cabin, and then make herself vomit in our trash can), but it was a very unhealthy environment – exactly what I needed to avoid at the time. The few weeks following the trip to Stanford were truly the first where rays of light started to bore through my thick skull into my brain. These rays made me question my affliction with the disease. *Should I start eating normally again?* For the prior seven years, I had not had this internal dialogue. Sure, there had been extremely rare, fleeting moments when I scared myself with how sick I was becoming, and consequently questioned whether I should increase calories just a little, but there were no true, sustained thoughts that crossed my mind. To be clear, it wasn't as if my mind was telling me "yes, let's definitely start eating" while my body, on autopilot, continued to restrict food. It was more like my usual behavior and thoughts of deprivation, running further and faster, and staying lean was peppered with increasingly frequent mind-chatter that maybe I had better change.

Katy's bulimia made me uncomfortable. The sounds of retching kept me up at night. I began wearing my headphones to try to block out the sounds of vomit plopping into the trash. Katy was so thin and pale, with bony knees that stuck out like a bulging mouse in a snake's digestive tract. Her teeth were browned and marbled from acid erosion, and she smelled like cleaning products. She would ride her bike up and down the hills I would run, looking like her legs would snap as she pressed down on the pedals, gritting her teeth in what I can only assume was pain.

Even when I confronted her about it, Katy would not admit to her issue. Ultimately, after the camp in email conversations, she did admit that she "had been bulimic in the past but was better," although I think her behavior at the camp would suggest otherwise. Part of being grossed out by Katy was obviously the vomiting, but the other part was that as I looked at her sickly, spindly body and weird behaviors, I was sort of looking into a mirror. I felt grossed out that my disease was associated with hers. We were not that much different, yet she made me nauseated.

36.
Anorexia Statistics

ORIGINALLY THOUGHT OF AS just a medical problem, anorexia nervosa was first classified as a psychiatric disorder by the American Psychiatric Association in 1980. Anorexia nervosa has varying definitions, depending on the medical dictionary. *Farlex Medical Dictionary* defines it as follows:

> Anorexia nervosa is a psychiatric disorder characterized by an unrealistic fear of weight gain, self-starvation, and conspicuous distortion of body image. The individual is obsessed with becoming increasingly thinner and limits food intake to the point where health is compromised. The disorder may be fatal. The name comes from two Latin words that mean "nervous inability to eat.[7]

According to the *Diagnostic and Statistical Manual for Mental Disorders, Fourth Edition*, anorexia nervosa is defined as:

> The refusal to maintain body weight about 85% of predicted, an intense fear of gaining weight, undue influence of body shape or weight on self-image, and missing at least 3 consecutive menstrual periods.[5]

Eating disorders are both a serious mental illness and highly prevalent. In fact, roughly 24 million Americans currently suffer from an eating disorder (anorexia, bulimia, or binge eating disorder).[13] The number of people diagnosed with anorexia has more than doubled since 1970, and this is thought to be a genuine increase in the prevalence, and not just an increase in reporting.[7]

111

Anorexia statistics are even more staggering for adolescents. 95% of those who have eating disorders are between the ages of 12 and 25.8, and the mortality rate associated with anorexia nervosa is 12 times higher than the death rate associated with all causes of death for females 15 to 24 years old.[7] While anorexia is a psychiatric disorder, it affects all organ systems of the body, principally the cardiovascular and endocrine systems. Complications can involve virtually any body system, including the gastrointestinal, renal, reproductive, neurologic, orofacial, dermatologic, and the hematologic systems. In fact, eating disorders have the highest mortality rate of any mental illness.[2]

Ninety percent of people with eating disorders are women.[12] 20% of people suffering from anorexia will die prematurely from complications related to their eating disorder, including suicide and heart problems.[12]

Elite athletes may be even more likely to suffer from an eating disorder. This is speculated to be the case because the typical psychological traits of anorexics and elite athletes are similar: perfectionism, high self-expectations, competitiveness, hyperactivity, repetitive exercise routines, compulsiveness, drive, tendency toward depression, body image distortion, pre-occupation with dieting and weight. Among athletes, those in aesthetic sports (gymnastics, ballet, figure skating) and endurance sports (long distance running and cross country skiing) are significantly more likely to develop eating disorders compared to non-athletic peers. Lastly, studies show higher rates of eating disorder in elite athletes over peers (9% to 20%).[11]

Research has not been conclusive on the causes of anorexia. It has been linked to genetics as well as biological, psychological, and social factors. However, compared to many other diseases, the genetic component does not appear to be as strong. Even so, twin studies show that if one twin has anorexia nervosa, the other has a greater likelihood of developing the disorder, and studies have shown that having a close female relative with anorexia nervosa also increases the likelihood of other female family members developing the disorder. There may be variations of the 5HTT (serotonin transporter gene) genome that are associated with the development of various eating disorders.[10]

Similar to other mental disorders such as depression, some evidence indicates that anorexia is linked to abnormal neurotransmitter activity. Anorexics may have a defect in the part of the brain that controls pleasure and appetite, although studies in this arena are new to the fore and inconclusive to date.[8]

Psychological factors, specifically certain personality types, appear to play an important role in developing the disease. Anorexics tend to be perfectionists who have unrealistic expectations about how they "should" look and perform. They tend to have a black-or-white, right-or-wrong, all-or-nothing way of seeing situations, and have difficulty resolving conflicts. Many anorectics lack a strong sense of identity and instead take their identity from pleasing others. Virtually all anorexics have low-self worth, low self-esteem, and difficulty communicating negative emotions. Many experience depression and anxiety disorders, although researchers do not know if this is a cause or a result of the eating disorder.[8]

Research has identified social factors that increase the likelihood of developing anorexia. Besides the pervasive media messages that thin people are more successful and deserving than fat people, anorexics tend to come from families that honor high, unrealistic, and/or rigid expectations. Anorexics are more likely to come either from overprotective families or disordered families where there is a lot of conflict and inconsistency. Both of these situations lead the individual to want to control something – and this becomes body weight in the case of anorexia.

Very often something stressful or upsetting triggers the start of anorexic behaviors, ranging from seemingly simple conflicts such as being teased about body weight or comparing the person unfavorably to someone thin, to bigger life events such as moving or a death in the family.[7] Similarly, many social situations play into the development of anorexia from an initial diet and exercise program. If a mildly overweight or normal weight individual (particularly a teenage female) loses some weight on a diet, she may receive initial positive reinforcement for this behavior, such as compliments by peers on her appearance. This reward may be highly important to this individual (based on her personality type, age, and social factors), which can cause an inability to stop this behavior once ideal body weight is achieved.[8]

Anorexia Athletica (aka Sports Anorexia and Hypergymnasia) is not formally its own mental health disorder but is recognized in the psychiatric community as a distinct eating disorder. The disorder refers to "a disorder for athletes who engage in at least one unhealthy method of weight control."[14] It is often characterized by excessive, obsessive exercise, frequently accompanied by caloric restriction. It is most commonly found in pre-professional and elite athletes, particularly those involved in sports where a lean body is advantageous, such as distance running. Anorexia Athletica sounds a lot like what I suffered from. Although concern may be present about the size and shape of the body, the most hallmark criteria is that self-worth is tied to physical performance and how lean a person is compared to his or her successful or professional counterparts. The focus is on performance rather than body image.[6]

This description very accurately describes the later years of my disease. I did not care how much I weighed, and I did not even think I was fat (as is often the case with anorexics). My focus was on being a world-class runner. My entire identity rested on my success in each given race or workout: I was not a student, not a younger sister, not a daughter, not a friend, not a compassionate person, not someone with a sense of humor – I was an excellent runner.

Anorexia Athletica is thought to spiral into obsessive behavior, wherein the athlete only gets a sense of control over their body through over-exercising and under-eating. This may initially stem from coaches or parents pressuring the athletes to improve performance by encouraging increased exercise, training, or dieting. Athletes usually begin by eating more "healthy" foods as well as increasing their training, but when this brings modest improvements in performance, they may feel that is not enough, and start exercising excessively and cutting back caloric intake until it becomes an obsessive psychological disorder. Anorexia Athletica is central in the Female Athlete Triad: low energy availability (eating disorders), amenorrhea (menstrual dysfunction), and bone density loss (osteoporosis).[6]

Initially, I suffered from Anorexia Nervosa because I was not yet running (or regularly exercising) at the young age of ten when the disorder began. As I started running more and flourishing on the success I was having, the disorder shifted and became more aligned with Anorexia Athletica.

Sayer Sisters, 1989 From Left: Ashleigh, Amber, Emily

Amber, age 10, in Nantucket leading a few ducks on the beach

Amber, age 12, after finishing
10th in her first cross country race

Amber, age 13, after Junior Olympic
National Championships in
Spartanburg, SC

Amber, age 13, attempting to throw the shot put after winning a trip to the USA Track & Field Trials

Amber, age 14, at Kinhaven Music Camp

Amber, age 15, and teammate Nora, after the Western Massachusetts Track & Field Championships after shattering the 11:00 mark in the 2-mile

Amber, age 15, sporting her Girl Scout vest

Amber, age 15, during a cross country race on her home course at Amherst
Regional High School
*Photo courtesy of Alison Wade

Amber, age 16, and her father
and family dog in Washington
D.C. to tour Georgetown
University prior to Penn Relays

Amber, age 16, with her mother enjoying a side trip to San Francisco,
while out in California for USA Junior Nationals

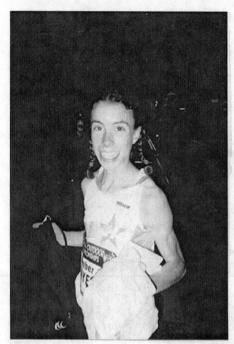

Amber, age 16, after running the 5000m in 17:07 at the USA Junior Nationals in Palo Alto, CA

Amber, age 17, talking to a reporter after a cross country race during her senior year of high school

Amber, age 17, with her parents in New York City for the National
Wendy's High School Heisman Award Weekend

Amber and Ben on their wedding day, August 2012

37.
How Many Rolls can I Get With a Dollar?

ABOUT A MONTH AFTER the trip to Stanford and three weeks after I learned I had qualified, it was time for the trip to Barbados for the Junior Pan American Games. I ran 17:46, good for the Bronze medal, which I was happy enough with given the tropical heat and humidity. The bizarre thing about the race was that in the last few laps, all I could think was, *I'm hungry*. I did not usually feel hungry before races, because I fueled well before them with plenty of calories. Race days (or the nights before) were actually probably the biggest splurge days, so that I would have plenty of energy to run fast. The evening before a big race, I usually indulged in a large serving of pasta with marinara sauce, a big salad, a thick slab of fresh bread, and a small bowl of frozen yogurt. The fight to be thin never beat the fight to be fast, and I knew that in order to race well, I needed the fuel.

The decision to finally change became cemented in my mind during my trip to Barbados. I felt worn down, weak, hungry, and scared. Above all, I felt empty. One night, I was sitting around the track watching events with the team's sports psychologist, Dave Templin. At the time, I didn't know that this was his role on the team (I thought he was an athletic trainer until I recently Googled his name and found the original roster for Team USA, which included his title). I befriended him during the trip because I was one of the youngest runners and had no family there. Most of the other high school athletes traveled with droves of family members – parents, siblings, aunts, grandmas, and cousins. I was there all by myself and yearned for some parental support. Dave swooped into that role and, not to sound overly dramatic, but I owe my life to him.

Over the duration of the trip, Dave and I sat and watched all the races together. He talked about his wife and their new baby back home. He asked me about my family, how I got into running, and what it was I liked about the sport. We would watch the events and talk to pass the time. The food on the trip was terrible – some catered food that was unrecognizable, and Dave always complained that he was hungry. It is in my nature to nurture and to try to help people that I care about, and I started to care about Dave quickly. He reminded me of my Uncle Roger and made me feel like I had a fan there, even though I did not come with anyone.

In the mornings, I would walk down the big hill to the market and buy ingredients, then walk back up to University campus where we were staying. The dorm had a small kitchen, so I would put together little meals in Tupperware containers – pastas, salads, and wraps. Nothing fancy, but something homier than the catered gray sludge that was presented in large tin trays. I brought the meals to the track and gave them to him. One night he mentioned that he missed bread and wished he could sink his teeth into some kind of roll. Thanks to spending over an hour a day running around Barbados that trip, I knew the perfect bakery and walked there. It was much further than I thought it was, because running is vastly more efficient than walking, and I misjudged how long it would take. I eventually made it to the bakery and purchased half a dozen fresh rolls for a dollar.

On the walk back, the night was still. It was late July on a tropical island: hot and humid, with a big, bright moon illuminating the little homes. I had a plastic bag of warm rolls, my thoughts, and a familiar gnawing in my stomach. I longed for someone to talk to, someone to hug me. The sounds of my footsteps on the quiet street were my only company. I thought about my parents back home and how I wished they were there. Out loud into the empty night, I said, "I miss you Mom." She had always accompanied me to my big races, and without her I felt fractured. I thought about how I missed Ashleigh and how Emily would be moving to Chicago to start college in a few weeks. I was missing one of the last weeks we'd all live under the same roof.

I realized that even if I had the means to make international calls at the payphone, I didn't have any real friends who would be happy to hear from me. By avoiding social events at school, being obsessed with running and wanting to avoid eating at all costs, I had alienated most of my friends. I was enshrouded in a blanket of loneliness. My hand, as if independent from my brain, reached into the bag of rolls. Before I knew it, I was eating one – a completely foreign concept for such a late hour of the night and for being alone. I always tried to eat calorically-dense foods in the presence of others, so as to keep suspicions of my eating disorder at bay. The roll was flaky and still warm, breathing moisture into the bag in a glistening steam. My heart started racing faster when I realized what I was doing, but I also felt a sense of internal peace.

As the road stretched on, I started to be able to make out the stadium in the distance. Civilization seemed within reach again. When I finally made it back to my seat next to Dave, there were only two rolls left. I handed them to him and said, "This should help you feel better." He smiled and said, "You should have one too."

"I did. These are yours." It was a powerful moment, because my statement was honest. I had eaten four rolls. We sat and talked, watching the final heats of the night. I forgot all about how I had consumed the rolls. I told him about how I missed my family and felt really lonely inside. He told me he was there for me and that when I got home, I should tell my family that I need them.

The rest of the trip was mostly uneventful. I spent time with Dave, whose advice managed to seep into my brain and affect me more than anyone else's had in the past. Something about our conversations and what he made me realize about what was happening in my life made me want to get healthy again. I wanted to have a life that was more fulfilling, one with human connection, and one with less pain.

I still wear my Team USA gear with pride and look to Dave occasionally for his unparalleled sports wisdom, mental techniques, and advice about life. Earning the Bronze medal was a huge accomplishment and one I always will cherish. It marked an incredible opportunity to proudly represent my country, and an honor I had earned through hard work. Even so, I will remember it mostly for being the moment my disease broke open – where I became ready to change.

38.
Weight Re-gain

IT WASN'T A FLAWLESS turnaround to regular healthy eating when I got back to Massachusetts after my experience in Barbados. I started consuming a much wider variety of foods, adding options back into my diet that I had completely avoided while the anorexia was most severe. Since we lived in a very low-fat, vegetarian household, I still ate very healthfully, but with larger portions and less-restricted choices. I ate the whole veggie burger at dinner, rather than hiding half of it. I had a full mug of ice cream before bed, rather than as little as I could get away with. For lunch, I stopped bringing just spinach salad. Instead, I started bringing peanut butter and banana sandwiches on bread we made at home, and eating the whole thing. I ate Clif Bars between classes, dried apple rings and roasted almonds before practice, and drank my full glass of milk with dinner.

There were two major issues. The first was that while I think my parents could tell I was eating a lot more, I had been cheating for so many years and with such a substantial amount of weight on my dishonest weigh-ins that by the end, I managed to manipulate the scale to read 16 pounds more than I actually weighed. Sixteen pounds is a lot of weight for someone of such a tiny size, so in order to show my mom that the new me was gaining weight, I could only cheat less per week. I was scared to tell the whole truth all at once, because I didn't want to be punished for my prior dishonest behavior.

I'm not sure what my mom would have said if I'd sat down with her and had an honest, heart-to-heart confession, telling her that I had cheated all those years, particularly in the previous few months, and that I was much lighter than she thought but now was actually gaining weight and getting better. As an adult who has gained wisdom as I've matured, and who knows my mother better now than I did then, I believe she may have respected my honesty and worked with me to monitor my weight gain in a now-truthful fashion, even if I was frighteningly light. At the time, I was too ashamed and cowardly to admit my sinful behavior. It felt like I had dug myself a huge hole, and there was no other way to climb out. As weight came back on, I would gradually "cheat less" on weigh-in day. This deceitful behavior regularly reminded me of how low I had sunk during my disease: I was not the girl I wanted to be.

The second point of note is that weight gain occurred very rapidly. Because I had essentially destroyed my metabolism over nearly eight years of starvation, my body had become accustomed to surviving on very few calories. Eating anything over about 800 calories at this point resulted in weight gain. In the spring of my junior year, I was eating an average of 500-800 calories per day, depending on my training schedule (and I ran between 10-15 miles daily), and was now eating about 3,000 calories while running half as much. On average, once I started eating again, I gained about two pounds each week – which was the rate that the pediatrician was hoping I could achieve. However, it is important to note that although this was medically recommended, it is a very aggressive pace, yielding eight pounds of weight per month. That amount of weight gain will be stored nearly entirely as body fat, because it is simply impossible to gain appreciable muscle mass that quickly.

39.
Overeating in High School

SOME DAYS, THE BIOLOGICAL urge to get calories into my body became such a loud scream that it was impossible to muster enough willpower to ignore it, even when I wanted to. My body was demanding food and even if I had just eaten a meal, I was ravenous for calories. This filled me with a sense of repulsion toward myself, as well as severe social anxiety. I worried that people would think I was now bulimic, given how much I was packing down; or worse, just disgustingly fat. (Even though I was barely seventy-five pounds by the beginning of senior year, I felt that people would view me as fat.)

One day just before Thanksgiving of my senior year, I was sitting in calculus class and so hungry I couldn't even hear. I would like to differentiate this from "listen." My body was yelling so loud for food that I literally could not hear human language around me. When the bell rang, instead of going to English class, I walked out the front door of the school. I got in my car in a frenzied panic to get food at home. I sped out of the parking lot, right through a two-way-stop, sideswiping another car and crashing into a stop sign. My car was totaled. My heart was racing at the sound of the impact. *I could have hurt someone.* Luckily, the woman was physically fine, as was I. When my mom came after the police called her, I lied and said that I had forgotten an assignment at home and was rushing home to retrieve it before class. I felt too disgusting to tell her I was so ravenous that I had to skip class to go eat food.

Another interesting thing happened due to this uncontrollable urge to eat. I began hiding food again. Not food I had supposedly eaten, as I had during the anorexic days, but food I wanted later when no one was looking: chocolates in my shoe hanging bag, pretzels between my bed and the window, protein bars in my oboe case. These were the safety rations I could eat when I had privacy and I had to get fuel.

I could not get enough food, and I was desperate to eat the minute the feeling of hunger came knocking. If I tried to ignore the urge, I became dizzy, headachy, and felt like I had fallen under a spell. Something other than my own mind would drive me to eat, like a puppet master controlling my hands and mouth. When I was in school, sometimes all I could think about was food. Even though I had always been a top-achieving student, I would now completely space out when teachers called on me. I lived in fear of not being able to get my next meal. It was a complete one-eighty from just months before.

40.
The Dark Side of the Spotlight

THE TROUBLE WITH EVERYONE in Amherst knowing me through my job at Hastings and my picture appearing in the paper every week after races, was that after my recovery began and I slowed down, people started asking me why I wasn't running as well, expecting the same stellar results. As injuries set in, I was constantly asked about them, which simply served to rub it in that I wouldn't be able to run until the injury healed. I couldn't escape the disappointed looks when I mentioned I had to sit out a race because I was injured, or that so-and-so beat me at a big invitational. My face must have been flushed with embarrassment and shame every shift that I worked.

Some locals wanted to offer their "solutions" to my "running plateau." One day, one of the usual Sunday morning customers came in for his paper. "How was the race, champ?" he asked. "Eh, I did alright." "You know, I think you've put on a little weight. It's probably slowing you down." I tried to remain stoic and politely nod, as if to say, "good idea." A lump filled my throat as I fought back tears. *I did gain weight. I'm fat now. I'll never be fast again.* When he left, tears filled my lower eyelids, hanging on by surface tension alone, ready to spill over if I turned my head too quickly.

My boss came over and put her hand on my shoulder. "Why don't you take a few minutes," she offered. I went upstairs to the bathroom, bolted the old-fashioned lock, and melted into a pile of tears on the wooden floor. After a few minutes of collecting myself, I stood up and looked in the mirror. My face was red and splotchy. I lifted up my shirt and stared at my reflection in the mirror. *Where are your ribs? You're disgusting.* I felt that because I could finally pinch some skin and get some fat in there, I was obese. (I was not - I was barely 85 pounds, which, at five feet, is still underweight).

Ultimately, it was challenging to get over the eating disorder when I grew up in a small town where everyone knew me either by name, or as "that crazy fast runner girl." In addition to feeling like I let people down as I gained weight and slowed down over my senior year, this notion was constantly on my mind during about fifteen hours of conversations with customers at work each week, and therefore was very hard to ignore. My self-esteem was Mariana Trench-low. I no longer had an identity. I was no longer as successful as I had been when I was younger, and wasn't impressive to others or myself. In my "glory days," I felt like I was a ray of hope for some townies, representing Amherst (a town that residents seem to have an abnormally great pride to live in). These problems are tough for an individual - the inner dialogue in one's mind, the pervasive feeling that you are failing. For me, it was magnified by several hundred people - all of whom I felt I had also let down. I felt bad for disappointing Amherst. My hometown folk were no longer proud of me. Sometimes I felt even *they* were embarrassed by my performances.

41.
Heisman Award

NEAR THE END OF fall during my senior year, I received a nomination for the Wendy's High School Heisman award. I am actually still not sure who nominated me, but a student can receive a nomination from a teacher or faculty member at his or her high school. The award recognizes high-achieving seniors who excel academically and athletically, and have a positive impact on the community through leadership and service. I had never heard of the award, but upon nomination, I soon learned of the award process and the prestige.

After a student is nominated, he or she fills out an application and writes an essay. From these applicants, one winner is chosen from each school. Ten males and ten females are crowned state finalists from each state from the pool of school winners. The best male and female applicant is selected from this pool and awarded the state title at an award ceremony. As the Massachusetts winner, I was invited to the ceremony at Gillette Stadium.

State winners are notified by phone, and then a video crew is sent to their hometown to interview the student and film him or her in action for a day. I have always been shy, and while I enjoyed the glory of running well in races, I was intimidated by lots of attention or being in the spotlight. I was very nervous for the cameraman to follow me around for the day, because I knew other students would be staring at school and asking questions about why I was being filmed, and the same would hold true of people in all the other locations at which I was going to be filmed.

It turned out to be a rather painless process, and one in which I was reminded that people are just curious because they care, and most people are not interested in making fun of you. I was filmed in class giving a presentation, at practice running with teammates, at work at Hastings, and doing service work as I worked on my Girl Scout Gold Award. At home, I played oboe and was interviewed about my achievements, my experiences, and what I wanted to share about success.

The banquet at Gillette Stadium was on a Thursday night in November. After practice, my parents and I drove down, where we sat through a very long, vegetarian-unfriendly dinner. I ended up being crowned the Northeast Region female winner. Six female and six male regional winners were invited to the National Finals in New York City for a weekend of activities and ceremony during ESPN's national telecast of the college Heisman Trophy presentation.

The sad truth is that I felt undeserving of the award. I remember being shocked while sitting at the fancy table with my parents at Gillette when they called my name as the National Finalist, representing the Northeast Region. I was proud to earn $2,000 for my high school (the National Finalist's prize), but my self-image no longer correlated with that of a champion. It seemed innately backwards that I was winning such a comprehensive, prestigious award, because I did not feel like a success. *I am fat and slow; I am not a winner. Maybe this is a setup, so they can reveal that I am actually a failure.* I had even struggled academically (more than usual) my senior year, because I had incredible trouble focusing on school. I was fighting depression due to massive changes in my body, mind, relationships, perception of myself, and athletic ability.

The week before the trip down to New York City, my mom offered to buy me a winter coat that I could wear, because many of the activities were going to involve walking outside. "Thanks, Mom, but I have a coat." "You have a ski jacket, Am. You need an elegant coat so you feel beautiful and mature alongside the other finalists." *Beautiful and mature? I feel fat and amorphous; I'd rather hide under my ski jacket.* My parents, although always proud of my accomplishments, were particularly thrilled with this victory. At the time, I thought it was because I had not garnered nearly as many accolades over the fall after gaining the weight, so they were so happy to see me on the top again. In retrospect, I surmise that they were proud because it was an honor to receive such distinction and acknowledgement of my achievements beyond those of "just running." I'm sure my parents were glad that I was being recognized for shining on and off the field (or track), and hoping that this would help remind me that I was more than just a good runner: I was a stellar student, a leader in my community, and caring in my actions.

The coat memory sticks out prominently because I knew that when my mom offered to get me a new coat, especially one that promised to be "mature," she felt that this was a big event. We were a family of savers - the Sayers save. The least amount of money possible was allocated for clothing, and 95% of our "new" clothes were purchased at the used clothing store. The only items we ever purchased brand new were socks, underwear, gloves, slippers, and the L.L. Bean fleece pajamas I got when I was about nine (and continued to wear throughout high school, since I never grew out of them). A new jacket indicated that the award was a very big deal. However, I did not really want to be part of it. I felt like a loser. I was someone who *had* been a big deal, but I had lost it all through bowls of cereal, plates of pasta, peanut butter sandwiches, and ice cream. The "old" me deserved the award. Then I was a champion - a role model. *Now I'm an ugly failure.*

Mom did buy me a new coat. It was navy blue suede and faux fur. I was much smaller at this point than I felt. Body dismorphia was at an all-time high. I was too small to even fit into a woman's zero so we went with a girl's coat from JCPenney. In a girl's size fourteen, I felt like a woman's plus.

I remember sheepishly following the group of National Finalists around New York City, feeling like I wanted to hide in the back with my parents as the "winners" strutted around the sites in front of us (although, let's face it, the ski jacket would have made me stick out like a sore thumb in the sea of black pea coats everyone else wore). It was the first and only time I went to the top of the Empire State Building. Staring down at the city blanketed in

136

frosty, gray December air, I felt pain. I wanted my old life back – the life where I felt that everything was possible, that I was untouchable, and that I was in control of my own destiny. In my "old life," I knew I could have won. The only glimmer of pride I felt was briefly when my name and photo flashed in Times Square on the Coca Cola billboard, announcing my National Finalist status.

At the awards ceremony, they aired edited clips, sort of a "bio reel" from the films that were done in our hometowns. I turned red when they played mine in front of the other finalists, their families, and the rest of the audience. I felt like a fraud. Why would people think this girl was one of the best six in the nation? I did not end up winning the National title.

At the post-ceremony banquet, I stuffed my face with my sorrows in the form of chocolate petite fours. I must have had twenty over the course of the party. Occupying myself at the buffet line was a good way to avoid conversation, and the cakes tasted so good, I forgot how much pain I was in. 4,000 calories later in the hotel room that night, I said my prayers to God, asking him to help me get my life together. The irony is, my life was more together at that time than the life I was asking to get back.

42.
My Final Semester of High School

THE FINAL SEMESTER OF high school was extremely difficult for me on an emotional level. At this point, encumbered by all my new body fat, I was running pretty poorly. I had several serious physical injuries. However, the blow to my ego was the hardest. Because I had alienated the majority of my close friends during the anorexia, I was incredibly lonely. My sister Emily had moved to Chicago for college and, for the first time in my life, I was the only child at home. School was lonely; home was lonelier. The pressure over going to college became a reality. The schools that had been knocking down my door to recruit me all wanted the old me – the star athlete – and I had been focusing on getting into the school with the best track program. Although I was at the top of my class academically, I felt overwhelmed with the decision, because I no longer knew what I wanted out of college or out of life. Every customer at Hastings had his or her two cents about where I should go. An essay I wrote about being bombarded with the "where are you going to school?" question was even published in the local newspaper, but it didn't stop anyone from asking.

Through working at Hastings, I developed a close friendship with Ben, one of the first non-runner boys that I had ever had a relationship with as a teenager. I had a few male friends that I was friendly with at school, but no one that I was particularly close to who didn't run. This became increasingly important as my running caliber declined. Ben, my co-worker at Hastings, was two grades above me, and a long-time childhood friend of most of my closest male running friends who had also graduated. Ben was not an athlete, but played guitar in several bands. When I was a freshman in high school, his blue hair and crazy braids intimidated me. But as I got to know him while we worked together, I found that he was quite the contrary – an unbelievably sweet guy, the best listener, funny, and oozing kindness in the form of a once-in-a-lifetime quality friend.

With some time, Ben ultimately became my rock. Although my running had always impressed him, and he had been supportive and interested when I talked about it junior year, Ben became irreplaceable in his ability to see me as more than "just a fast runner." I was blessed that he was one of the few people who stuck around Amherst after graduating from the high school, attending the University of Massachusetts while most of his peers left for colleges in other parts of the country. In a way, we both had big holes to fill at the loss of our friends, and although we were not that close initially, it was only a month or two that everyone was gone before we both felt the emptiness. As our friendship grew, we hung out more and more outside of work. As I pushed people out of my life my junior year, something about Ben made me pull him in closer. He stuck with me at some of my lowest moments of the disease, when sometimes my brain was so starved for glucose that I was irrational, irritable, and consumed by running and eating.

As I gained weight and began the emotional and incredibly arduous recovery, Ben constantly reminded that I was so much more than a runner. Ben was not in the "running circle," and our entire relationship was based on everything besides running. Because of this, he saw me as a regular friend who also ran on the side - a component of my life that had nothing to do with his interactions or impressions of me. By allowing me to escape the pigeonhole that I myself, and everyone else, had put me in, Ben allowed me to imagine a more well-rounded life where I had other positive attributes as a human besides being fast.

Personal problems escalated at home throughout senior year, and I sunk into serious depression with an increasing lack of self-worth. Ben's companionship became the hand that kept me from going over the edge. A few times during an injury in my quadriceps, I went to hang out with him in his dorm instead of cross-training at the gym. He provided me with a much-needed hamlet away from training. We didn't do anything special; it was the company that was important, as well as the temporary escape from the world of running, eating, and self-judgment.

Ben taught me that I needed to take care of myself first and foremost, which sometimes meant distancing myself from the track for a day, kicking back and watching a TV show, and eating ice cream. He taught me that it was more important that I found a way to be happy than get my workout in at the gym, if on that given day the two were oppositional. Sometimes we just drove. I'd watch the streets of Amherst blur by through my window as I zoned out, imagining the days not long ago that it felt like I would run along them at the same pace as the car. In my "fat" body, I felt a stabbing pain to my heart and ego. I couldn't wait to graduate high school, because I just wanted to get away from the world that knew me as the "once super-fast" runner.

The truth is, my senior year, I was not suddenly a slow runner. I just lost my "elite" ranking and fell back a few pegs. I set the course record on our high school cross-country course and ran several good races that season. I even won the Western Mass Championships in Outdoor track, again in the two-mile, this time just jogging as fast as I needed to for the win (twelve-minutes flat) with a neoprene sleeve on my quad because of a muscle tear. In States the following week, I ran terribly – one of the last runners. I was limping, and in pain physically, mentally, and in my heart. It felt sort of like a depressing swan song – a former star limping slowly around the track in a body vaguely reminiscent of my old one, watching the new waves of emaciated runners lap me for the win.

43.
College Decision

THE COLLEGE APPLICATION PROCESS came at a very unfortunate time for me. I was heavily recruited as I reached my peak in my junior year track season. Colleges had been sending me pamphlets since the eighth grade, but in accordance with NCAA recruiting rules, phone calls from coaches started rolling in right after I finished my junior year. Because I was an extremely strong student academically, the list of college choices within arm's reach was essentially limitless. With two older sisters, I had already tagged along on numerous tours and had a decent sense of what various schools were like. The trouble was, although the process to actually go on official visits and start thinking seriously about applying began at the very peak of my high school running career, it was a short-lived period of time before my recovery began, and running turned from being everything to me, to being everything that was painful for me.

What this meant practically was that throughout my sophomore and junior years, I wanted a full scholarship to run at a competitive D1 school, where running was a big focus, with great coaches, successful athletes, and top-notch facilities. My top choice for quite some time had been Stanford, which fit this bill to a T. It also had the added advantage of being a great academic school in a more ideal climate than New England. I figured anywhere warmer would not have quite the struggle of training through New England winters on slippery snow-covered roads, in bone-chilling winds, and on very dark afternoons.

I liked all academic subjects in school, and to my credit, I was smart, disciplined about doing homework, and quite successful in class. Science had long been my favorite, so I knew I wanted to go to a school with strong science programs, but beyond that, I honestly had no idea what I wanted to do with my life. As a child, I entertained a number of dream jobs – from baker when I was four so I could "eat the doughnuts," to geologist in second grade because I was obsessed with collecting rocks, to teacher, veterinarian, engineer, and oncologist, among many others. However, the closer I became to needing to settle on a route, the less I dreamed. All I had wanted to be for the previous eight years was a world-class runner.

Another big criterion for my college choice throughout high school was that I wanted to go far away from home. The reasons for this changed as I changed. During the height of the anorexia, my relationship with my mother was incredibly strained. We were in a constant war over food, and I was more than ready to get out from under her watchful eye. I couldn't wait to be "on my own" to make my own choices and not be controlled by her. This was much less of an issue during my senior year, as our relationship was starting to slowly mend. However, I still desperately wanted to escape Amherst, to try and leave behind memories and build a new reputation through a fresh start.

College applications always had lines for inputting your extracurricular activities. Cross-country, track, Girl Scouts, oboe...as I was recovering, I felt like I should put "anorexia," as it had consumed more time than probably all of those combined – between up to three or four doctors visits a week, the time obsessing over food, learning about calories, fighting with my parents, and worrying.

I applied to Stanford early action, and then Duke, Rice, Princeton, Georgetown, Brown, and Williams regular decision. My application was deferred to normal admissions at Stanford, and I got into all of the other schools, with varying degrees of financial aid.

I chose Duke University. I thought it had a good blend of rigorous academics, an ideal climate, a solid distance from home, a competitive yet reasonable D1 program, and it lacked some of the "issues" I saw in other schools. In Amherst, I felt like a big fish in a small pond. I was tired of that. I wanted to slide further under the radar and be a small fish in the big pond of Duke. However, what I discovered was that I didn't even know how to swim. It was as if I hadn't been a big fish in small pond in Amherst, but rather a fish out of water - someone everyone recognized flapping about and struggling to breathe.

In retrospect, I truly wish I had chosen Williams College. This feeling didn't take eight years to arrive, either. I knew before my first day at Duke that Williams would have been a better choice, because by the time pre-season was about to start, I was a very different person with completely different goals and needs than the person I had been a few months before signing my acceptance decision letters.

I had originally not chosen Williams because it seemed much too small and in the middle of nowhere, where I feared life would be like high school all over again. On my recruiting trip, we went to a wild party where I was extremely uncomfortable, with dirty novelty cakes, inflated condoms, and tons of drinking. I was very straight-edge as a competitive runner and had "wholesome" friends in high school. At the party, I was tired and wanted to go back to the dorm, where I was staying with a girl on the team. She, however, was on the injured list. Because she was not competing, she was partying hard.

I wasn't allowed to leave the crazy gathering until she was partied out. That rule alone was enraging to me. What was worse, in the morning (I was always a morning person) I had to go to the bathroom so badly. My host was in such a deep hangover sleep that I couldn't wake her. Students had to access the dorm bathroom with a key that she had (and had neglected to tell me that, or where I could find the key). I tapped her so many times she might as well have been dead!

I ended up running barefoot out of the dorm and peeing in the bush out back. When I returned to the door, I found myself locked out of the dorm in the cold Western Massachusetts November morning. With my shoes still inside, frost soaked through my socks as I waited for someone to come out so I could get back in. College students aren't up at 6:30 on a Sunday morning. It was a long wait.

With all that said, I loved the coach at Williams. He reminded me of my uncle. The running program, while incredibly competitive for its division, was D3, so it would have been less intense than any of the other schools I applied to (which were all D1). D3 would have been a better fit for me, given my new, slower race times and focus on becoming healthy.

I wasn't wild about the coach at Princeton. I never actually visited Rice, Stanford turned me away (a blessing in disguise), and Brown had a weak financial package, although it still would have been a good choice. These facts ultimately led me to my decision to attend Duke.

Ultimately, the decision of Duke University was made rather hastily, sort of like "the best of the worst" choices. Even though there had been years of conversations with my parents about potential schools, dozens of visits, and excitement during earlier years in high school, when all the letters offering me a spot in the freshman class rolled in from several fantastic schools, I became largely non-communicative about the subject and tried to put the process off by ignoring the thoughts in my mind and avoiding the discussion with my parents and academic advisors. I had no idea what to do.

My mom offered to help me weigh pros and cons of each school, and while we tossed around some ideas, I usually kept most of the big, glaring concerns in my head. *Didn't they want me when I was fast? The coach probably forgot that I got the "you're in" letter and now wants me to turn them down.* I didn't want to disappoint my mom by verbalizing my fears. After all, I worried constantly that I was letting her down. I was no longer fast, I had no friends, no date to the prom, I'd started letting my grades slide at school, and I struggled tremendously to be an effective communicator, both at home and with my few friends. I simply missed out on learning how to express my emotions, ideas, and needs while I had been sick for the previous eight years. I only knew the internal dialogue in my own head. My mom remained patient with me and tried to reach out and support me as I waffled on the decisions.

Below is an email she sent me in late April of senior year (when the acceptance selection should have been fairly settled) demonstrating my evasion of the college selection subject:

Date: Thu, 22 Apr 2004 21:03:47 -0400

Thanks for the cool e-mail, I really enjoyed reading it. Incidentially. its great to see you smile and laugh these past couple days. You seem much more like yourself and much happier. I know that you are really trying hard with your running and your eating and it shows. You look wonderful and you are steadily running faster. So keep it up because the happiness really shows.

I.m not sure you have really dealt too much yet with college and that is as it should be for now. You had such a very long road to go down to get into college-it was long, and bumpy and pressured. Now I think you are just coasting. There is nothing that you really have to do yet. It is time to begin thinking about what it will be like though so you can start to mentally prepare for the changes, but thats all for now. Focus on wrapping up HS well and working on your running if thats what you want to do.

So take care. Be careful this weekend, Have a great track meet and know that I will be thinking about you. Love M*M
XXXXXXXXXXXXXXXXXXXXXXXXXXXXXXXXXXXXXXXXXXX
XXXXXXXXX

As the summer after my high school graduation progressed, I secretly regretted my decision. It felt too late to make any changes, and probably was, although I cannot say for sure. I was working at a sleep-away sports camp all summer and started to feel like I wanted to stay closer to home. In the privacy of my mind, I admitted to myself that I did not want to run for a D1 school because of the pressure, and because my running performance had severely declined. By the end of the summer, I also had a tibial stress fracture, which meant I would be entering the cross-country season injured.

44.
"Blue Devils"

I ARRIVED AT DUKE on August 9, 2005. Durham, North Carolina, was in the middle of a tropical storm. It was relentlessly pouring sheets of rain. All of the upper classmen were on their separate side of campus, and I was one of only three people on the entire freshman campus, two miles away.

That night I lay awake on the plastic-coated mattress without a cover sheet, in a soaking wet sleeping bag. My parents were going to be driving down the bulk of my linens and clothes for school when I returned from pre-season, so I had flown down by myself with just a backpack of stuff to get me through the first two weeks. The downpour had saturated all of my things, and since it was August, the automatic central air conditioner in the dorm room spouted icy air full-blast into my empty dorm room. Even with only the glow from stormy sky illuminating my room, I could see that my lips were purple. I was freezing. I went to the vending machine and bought Soft Batch Cookies. I ate the whole sleeve, then bought another and ate those. I called my mom. I called Ben. *What am I doing here? I want to come home.* In the nine months since I had visited Duke, I had gained another fifteen pounds and incurred several major injuries. Even worse, while eating disorders had not been obvious on my recruiting trip, it suddenly seemed like a very pervasive issue on the team.

The sinking feeling that Duke was the wrong school for me became even more obvious the next day, when our cross-country team traveled to Boone, North Carolina, for pre-season camp at Zap Fitness. Although Boone was an absolutely gorgeous town and my new teammates seemed like nice people, I was miserable at the camp. In addition to the fact that I was nursing an injury and was unable to run, the other girls on the team didn't eat. The first night, we were served arugula salad, steamed green beans, and baked chicken breast. As a lifelong vegetarian, I couldn't eat the chicken, and many of the girls also pushed it aside. "Mmmm. This food is delicious," one sophomore announced. "So filling." At the same table, each girl seemed to take a smaller serving than the previous, as if in a silent contest.

This was an incredibly toxic atmosphere for me to be in, because I was very unhappy with my "new" body (I say "new" body because my body looked and felt totally different after becoming 1.5 times its weight in one year). I was also starving. I was now accustomed to eating quite a substantial amount of food, and with nothing substantive available, I was hungry and weak. The one other freshman on the team was from Hawaii and had not yet arrived to Zap Fitness due to a plane delay. Because I was incredibly shy and was the obvious outsider, I kept to myself. None of the girls seemed interested in getting to know me. They gathered in one of the bedrooms and shut the door, giggling on the other side. Meanwhile I lay alone in my designated bed, staring at the ceiling, missing home.

Pre-season training camp set the tone for my first semester. Duke was a terrible fit. I felt intense pressure to fall back into my anorexic ways of denying my body nourishment and being obsessed with hours of exercise per day. Even though I was injured during cross-country season, those of us who were injured (and there were many of us) would cross train, usually twice a day for an hour at a time. I had a very hard time making friends because I was depressed, did not feel like putting myself out there, isolated myself every moment that I could, and in general felt like everyone around me was unlike me.

Students at Duke cared a lot about appearance: brands you wore, getting all made up for class, expensive shoes and handbags, jewelry. I had never cared about any of this. I was always a tomboy, even as a very young child. I liked to be dirty, wear comfortable clothes, and play adventurous games. I cared nothing about "girly" things. At my high school, this was not an issue. There were many like-minded peers. In fact, Amherst seems to be a perfect conglomeration of "weird" people. Very few people stick out, because there is not an obvious "normal."

My dormmates made fun of me. I wore "dorky" clothes and liked "dorky" things. I never wore makeup, and I wasn't obsessed with drinking or sex. I felt as if I had been transported to an alternate universe, the kind that seemed like a parody on television shows. Many of my peers had attended private schools and were very accustomed to being away from home. I was homesick. Their parents visited frequently, while mine only came once the entire year I was at Duke. They had private planes and timeshares in their families, attended debutant balls, and got storage units in Durham for their extra clothing.

I really felt like an oddball. Even the girls on the team made fun of me for being "rustic," whatever exactly they meant by that. They wore makeup to practice, had the latest sports clothing, and would go to the expensive dining hall after practice – which, with only $200 on my D-card (student card) for the year, was way out of my budget. I was not poor, but I certainly seemed like it compared to my peers. More than poor being the issue, I was simply "weird."

I did have a couple of saving graces at Duke. I made a few very good friends: Erin and Lindsey in my dorm and Rachel on my team, whose company I really enjoyed, even if they were very different than me. Ben and I stayed in touch. We grew closer and closer, talking most nights on the phone, and he helped me through some of the roughest, loneliest patches. However, I started weaning off my communications with my high school friends because they all seemed so happy at college and were thriving in their new environments while I was floundering. Additionally, at this point, I had fallen out of significant touch with my running friends from when I was younger.

My sister Emily was in a severe bike accident at school in Chicago, and although she thankfully survived, the incident caused me to have reoccurring nightmares that she died. I would wake up in the middle of the night, turn on my laptop, and Google "Emily Sayer Chicago" or "Emily Sayer bike accident." My heart would pound in my throat as I waited to see if any news articles would pop up alerting me that she was gone. When I was assured everything was okay, I'd get back in my bed and watch the clock crawl toward morning, eager for my roommate to wake up and end my loneliness.

45.
Rachel Umberger

MY CLOSEST FRIEND WHILE at Duke was Rachel Umberger, a middle distance runner on my track team. Rachel, who was from New Hampshire, was on the injured roster for the bulk of the year with me. I'm not sure if it was the New England in both of us, or perhaps a deeper connection based on well-matched personalities, but Rachel and I bonded during our hours of cross training. We typically rode the stationary bicycles together, pedaling out hard workouts and laughing at the weird people we would see at the gym. Rachel and I usually headed to the gym for our second session at 4:00 p.m. - the height of gym time - and watched the Ellen Show (something I had never even heard of prior to Duke). Even many of the non-athlete students at Duke appeared to be anorexic. Others would dress to the nines in fancy exercise clothes and talk loudly on the phone through their entire workout. We would laugh at the ridiculousness of the one-sided conversation we were privy to.

Rachel eventually confided in me that she suffered from uncontrolled bulimia, which had been a huge problem for her in high school, but would still flair up from time to time. She, like me, experienced her tremendous success in running while battling a massive eating disorder. In high school, Rachel had set many New Hampshire records in distances including the 600, 800, and 1,000m runs.

Rachel and I bonded over frustration that we were no longer nearly as fast as we once were. We both felt pressure to lose weight again, and felt out of control and unhappy with our lives. We had been stellar athletes for the vast majority of our lives and had become accustomed to that level of success. However, during this

150

time behind the scenes of what most people saw, we were fighting our demons to be incredibly thin. Our identity was our sport, and our self-identity was to stay ultra-lean running machines. Now we both hated running as well as ourselves for giving up the discipline we had possessed during the eating disorders. To realize that I hated no longer being able to make myself "be anorexic" is incredibly sad, but speaks volumes about the power of the disease and how anorexia completely takes over your mind and identity.

It was Rachel who helped me come to terms with the fact that Duke was probably not the best fit for me in the long term. She, like me, had not anticipated the magnitude of pressure we would feel to be thin again before attending, and felt that the team's environment was growing increasingly non-conducive to trying to get healthy. Because she was a year older than me, it was devastating for me to hear that she was still regretting her choice to attend Duke. I was hoping she would say it would get better. While I felt comforted to know someone was going through what I was, we were actually in different phases of our recovery, which put us at odds at times.

Ultimately, we both transferred and have since rekindled a healthy passion for running.

46.
"Run Big Red, Run"

WHEN I WENT ON my recruiting trip to Duke, I stayed the first night with Melissa Sangers[*] – another runner from Massachusetts, who was thriving as a sophomore on the team. Melissa had been the standout runner in Massachusetts before she graduated. She ran for Lexington High School in the eastern part of the state, clad in a yellow and blue uniform I can still picture. I always thought she looked like Julia Roberts; the guys on my team thought she was a goddess. She was incredibly thin with an angular nose, and I was sure that like me, she had an eating disorder. I had very little interaction with her prior to formerly meeting her at Duke.

On my recruiting trip, my suspicions of her eating habits were confirmed. She definitely did not eat enough. I spent the first 24 hours of the trip hungry and feeling like an obese walrus in my newly healthy-weight body. *A year ago, I would have loved this.*

The second night, I stayed with a different sophomore named Sally Meyerhoff. Sally was a bright, bold redhead with a personality as fiery as her hair. Her nickname was "Big Red." She was a top runner on the Duke team and hailed from Arizona. What was different about Sally compared to all of the other "more-elite-than-me" runners I had ever met, is that Sally ate. The first afternoon she took me to Cold Stone Creamery and we had ice cream. At dinner that night, she filled her plate with "normal" foods in contrast to the stark diet foods most runners subsisted on. Sally was fun and bubbly, sporting leopard prints and flashy pink clothing that mirrored her personality. When she took me to practice, she ran with me, introducing me to everyone and keeping

[*] Name changed

me entertained with hilarious stories as we traversed twelve miles through the Duke Forest.

When I was a student at Duke, Sally's love of food and life was a welcome breath of fresh air from the atmosphere of constant food deprivation and the almost unspoken "who can eat less than whom" contest, which was otherwise ubiquitous on the team.

One of my favorite memories with Sally was the Relay for Life night. Four of us teamed up to walk through the night to raise money for cancer research. Sally and I stocked up in advance with a big bag of chocolate-covered animal crackers. We snacked on dozens of the sinful treats while we walked, talking about our lives as well as those of the people we had known and loved with cancer. I felt safe with her; like I could be me – a girl that apparently loved to stuff her face with treats – and still probably be a fast runner. Sally was one of the absolute best on the team, and she loved to eat everything.

After I left Duke, I stayed in touch with Sally. We emailed back and forth a couple times per year, and I followed her running blog as she blossomed into a professional runner and triathlete after graduating. She was an inspiration to me. Her words were full of positive effects, motivational quotes, and true heartfelt stories of her runs and races that I could relate to. Sally was healthy and succeeding. She represented exactly what I wanted to be.

On March 8, 2011, Sally was killed riding her bike when she was struck by a truck driver at an intersection. The morning of the 9th, I was in Amherst, lying in the bed I grew up in. I read the story from my laptop in disbelief. *Dead?!* I verified it on a few sites. I ran down the hallway to my mom's room as tears rolled off my cheeks onto the hallway rug. "Mom! Sally...died." I could barely get the sentence out.

The loss of Sally still rattles me. I miss her words of wisdom, her smile, and the message she sent to the female running community – that you can be a powerhouse on the race course and still have a healthy attitude toward food. There needs to be more strong women, rather than skeletally thin women, that break the tape. Girls have posters of their running idols taped to their bedroom walls. How much healthier would their attitude toward running and food nourishment be if their role model had a muscular yet lean body? Our subconscious devours everything around us. Constant images of unnaturally thin runners can sink into your brain. As you push during a workout, trying to hammer out another repeat, what comes into your mind is the picture of your emaciated idol. *If she can do it, so can I.* You visualize how hard she must train and finish your workout hard. My opinion is we need more role models like Sally: young women with relentlessly positive attitudes, who train like beasts, but know how to live and enjoy a healthy life as well.

Because distance runners are often high achievers, they are willing to do anything and make all sacrifices to improve. There often becomes a mentality that it *should* be painful and hard, or you aren't doing enough. Athletes want to optimize their bodies, and there is a very fine line between healthy with low body fat and sickly emaciated. There is an even finer line between careful, clean eating and an eating disorder. In fact, there is a new term coined in just the last decade called "orthorexia." Orthorexia is essentially an obsession with eating healthy food. Like anorexia, it is also classified as a mental illness. Orthorexics avoid anything they perceive as being "unhealthy," which can often lead to malnutrition, social isolation, and behaviors similar to obsession compulsive disorder (OCD).

47.
Just a Casual Brunch

As I MENTIONED EARLIER, when I was at Duke University, freshmen lived on a separate campus than upper classmen. The campuses were about two miles apart, and busses ran between them. The freshman campus had its own dorms, library, dining hall, and several academic buildings. There was only one other freshman on the cross country team, Tia, and our schedules rarely overlapped.

On Sundays, the dining hall served brunch rather than breakfast. The dining hall was only open from 10 to 12, and then stayed closed until 6pm. I was usually one of the first people on the steps raring to get in, because I had been up for five hours and pushed through a two-hour practice on the other side of campus. As soon as the doors opened, I was like a desperate caged lion released into a pen of antelope. College students sleep late and Tia did not eat brunch, so I lacked friends as well as friendly company of any sort for 10:00 breakfasts on Sunday mornings. By myself, I would fill my tray with the things I liked. I still ate relatively healthfully, but way too much. I'd venture to say, I ate enough calories at Sunday breakfast to sustain a normal person for three days.

I ate fruit, such as watermelon and pineapple, I'd put down several bowls of cereal, and I'd dip Cracklin' Oat Bran cereal in a big scoop of peanut better. Then I'd move on to junk food. There was a frozen yogurt machine, and ice cream had always been one of my childhood favorites. There were probably only a handful of trips to the dining hall that year that did not include a soft-serve sundae. Sunday brunches came with a chocolate fountain, so then I'd fill a bowl with warm, melted dark chocolate and dunk strawberries and graham crackers in it. Lastly, I'd head to the dessert window and eat the icing off several slices of cake. The cake with the coconut frosting was my absolute favorite.

When all was said and done, I'd leave about an hour later with a pounding headache and a stomach so distended that I could barely walk. I'd waddle back to my dorm and slip in quietly, so as to not wake my roommate, who was still fast asleep. I would lie in bed, listening to the movie she had on repeat all night, and wait for the pain to die down. Luckily, the dining hall would not reopen for nearly seven hours – plenty of time for me to regain my voracious appetite.

There were a few freshmen that I'd see in the dining hall that clearly had eating disorders. The coxswain of the crew team will forever be emblazoned in my brain. She was severely anorexic, and I found it disgusting. In hindsight, I was probably jealous that unlike me at this point, she was able to be so incredibly restrictive in her dietary intake, but I remember cringing when she'd get up with her tray after consuming a single hard-boiled egg white, her arms only as wide as the bones within them.

With all this eating, it's understandable that even with hours of cross training every day for practice, I still gained weight quickly. The incredible caloric intake, coupled with the damage I had caused to my metabolism during years of starvation, caused this gain to be substantial. I put on about eighteen pounds over the academic year. This may not sound like much, but for someone who was barely five feet tall, this weight almost looks like wearing a fat suit.

By the time I arrived at Duke, my doctors had informed me that I was up to my healthy maintenance weight of one hundred pounds. That represented about a thirty-four pound gain over the preceding calendar year (summer of junior year to end of summer after senior year). This gain was exactly what my doctors had hoped to see, and by the time I arrived at preseason camp, I was at my body's "ideal weight." However, because I am of very short stature and have a petite frame, thirty-four pounds was over half of my weight at the time the re-feeding period began (when I was about 66 pounds). At the end of the first year of recovery, I was one and a half times my weight at the turning point in Barbados. Thirty-four pounds is a lot for any body to gain in one year and adapt to safely. As a result, particularly because I was still running a lot as well as trying to compete, my body broke down. Injury after injury plagued me that year. The worst were stress fractures, but I also had tendonitis, shin splints, and a partial tear of one of my quadriceps muscles during spring outdoor track season.

Body Mass Index (BMI) is often used as a measure of healthy body weight versus obesity, albeit with some inherent fallacies. A BMI under 18.5 is considered underweight, normal BMI is between 18.5 and 24.9, 25 to 30 is an overweight person, and a BMI greater than 30 is considered obese. At the end of the anorexia, I had a BMI of 13.7. This is severely underweight. But by the end of my freshmen year my BMI was up to 23.4, pushing the upper limit of the "normal weight category" and nearly in the designated overweight category.

While the weight gain over my senior year of high school was challenging on my body and mind, it was ultimately necessary in order to achieve a healthy weight for my body. In contrast, the eighteen pounds I gained during freshmen year at Duke was unnecessary. Although I grew a full inch and a bit more, it was all excess weight at that point – not putting me over the line into "overweight," but certainly heavy for a runner.

48.
Amherst Becomes Home Again

ABOUT TWO WEEKS BEFORE it was time to go back to Duke for my sophomore year, I panicked. I could *not* go back. I had been attending an organic chemistry course at the University of Massachusetts back in my hometown of Amherst all summer. Somewhere between the peaceful hillsides and my distillation labs, I decided that UMass would be a better fit. I contacted the cross-country coach, Julie LaFreniere, who helped expedite my admission. After some rushed paperwork, I withdrew from Duke and enrolled in UMass' kinesiology program.

Even after I transferred from Duke to the University of Massachusetts, I continued to struggle with running. There's no way to sugar-coat it – I was nowhere near as fast as I was in high school. Not only did that fill me with a sense of guilt that I was a recruiter's nightmare, but it shattered my self-esteem. It's very depressing to feel like you've already passed your peak by the age of eighteen. I felt like I had already been the best I was ever going to be, and it was all downhill from there. Moreover, I could not run more than about three or four months without incurring a fairly major injury. The more injuries, the more time I spent not running, which meant I got further from my fast days.

My college sophomore year (my first year at UMass), I stood back in the shadows, feeling like I had let Julie down after she pulled strings so I could be admitted to UMass at such a late date. But Julie understood where I was coming from. She was sympathetic to my situation, and said she even remembered when I was a tiny "skeletal-looking" runner, charging through campus when I was in high school. She said I ran so effortlessly, but she knew it was only a matter of time until it all fell apart. She was right.

Julie cared that I worked hard, had a good attitude, and tried to be a positive influence on my other teammates. Because I refrained from drinking, partying, and other such activities, she appreciated that I tried to impart this on my teammates, whose partying had been problematic in previous years. By the spring of my sophomore year, I greatly respected her. While Julie's training philosophies were different than the ones I had grown up on and flourished under, she had faith in me that I was going to improve again, and that meant the world to me.

The summer going into my junior year of college, I decided I would buckle down and try to train consistently and with purpose. My goal was to be fast again while staying healthy. By the time cross-country season began, I was running much better. Things started to improve slowly. I was running a little more dependably and finishing most races in second place on my team.

Julie was amazingly supportive. After a few weeks, I was showing promise, displaying strong leadership, and was finally smiling and coming out of my shell. Julie pulled me aside. She explained that there were extra funds for a scholarship that had been allocated to another runner who had been removed from the team. She offered me a full scholarship, retroactive to the beginning of the school year. It was the biggest vote of confidence anyone had given me in years. She was proud of my efforts and believed in me so much that she wanted to give me money for my education. My mom was thrilled. I felt like a champion again. I was a Division 1 scholarship athlete that had earned the scholarship *during* college, not in my heyday.

I ran pretty well throughout junior year. Although I battled a few minor injuries, I stuck with it and slowly improved my times. I became good friends with the top runner on my team, a girl from Long Island named Christina, and I enjoyed running again. I felt like she welcomed my company on long runs, and since we were both majoring in kinesiology, we had many classes together. I finally had a running friend again.

Christina's race times at UMass were on par with mine from high school. There were certainly days I had to fight jealously because she was so much thinner and more successful than I was in college, where it really mattered. She was bubbly and happy and won many races, awards, and honors. The brain does not forget, even if the body does. *You used to be that fast. In high school you would have been running these repeats forty-five seconds faster than this.*

Some nights I would dream that I was flying along, the way I did in high school. This hope was dashed when I awoke to look down at my body, which now looked like it had swallowed my high school body whole. It was during these times that I probably had an even more distorted body image than I did in high school. I felt like a gorilla in a fat suit. While I had been on the heavy side by the end of my year at Duke (where I ate the freshmen dining hall out of house and home), by junior year, I had slimmed down to a healthier-sized body for my height of 5'1" at about 112 pounds. For a distance runner, this is may be a bit heavy, but for a normal young adult, it is perfectly healthy.

My self-esteem stayed very low, even as my running improved. We had some family problems, and on top of that, I felt incredibly ugly, fat, and unlovable. It felt like all judgmental eyes were on me when I entered a room. Some of my teammates made fun of me for "being weird," and I was ashamed of the body I walked around in.

One night as I was leaving school, I walked down the campus' icy hill to the far cinder lot where I parked my car. I slipped on the ice and fell to the ground, cutting my lip. People stared, but no one said anything. I was freezing, soaked, and covered in slush. Moreover, I had nothing to look forward to. I was living at home and wasn't getting along well with my mom. When I finally made it to my car, the windshield was covered in snow and ice. Without a scraper, I used the side of my mitten to scrape the snow away as I turned on the engine to try and expedite the defrosting. I sat in winter's silence in my car, waiting for the remainder of the ice to melt. I was lonelier than I had ever been. The lot was desolate. I stared down at my fat lap and cried. I pinched the fat that clung to my body roughly until it hurt. I yelled into the frozen night, "I hate you!"

I was promoted to team co-captain with Ms. Speedy Christina for my senior year. The team underwent major changes because many runners who were still eligible decided not to run senior year. We also had a lot of young blood, and the team had a fresh new feel. I ran decently but still longed for the old days. I never asked my mom to come to a race in college. I was ashamed at how slowly I was running and was afraid to see disappointment on her face when I finished far from the front of the crowd. Each time I stood on the starting line, I had to hold back tears that she wasn't there. I missed the old days when I was proud of what I could do. In hindsight, I'm sure my mom wished I had invited her, and would have gladly come, proud that I was out there doing my best. I simply lacked the confidence to understand that, and still felt that I didn't deserve her love after being an anorexic burden.

49.
Commencement

BY THE FALL OF senior year, I was sick of school. I felt trapped in Amherst, stuck in a rut, and I longed for a change in my life. I was ready to move on, much like I did at the end of my senior year of high school. I had enough credits to graduate early, so I decided to move to New York City and get a job in the fitness industry. Within a week, I had interviewed with numerous gyms and found a room to sublet in an apartment in Harlem for $600 a month. The job I took was at a residential gym in Times Square, where I worked the 3 p.m. to 12 a.m. shift. Unfortunately, getting home at 1:00 in the morning in my neighborhood was no picnic.

It was the first time since I had started running that I took a total, prolonged break from the sport. Even through injuries, I had taken time off, but I always exercised in whatever other ways that I could.

I was surprised to find that I loved the break. I thought it would drive me nuts, but after a week or so, I was used to it. I didn't have much time to easily fit training into my schedule anyway, and I was spending almost all of my free time with Ben, who didn't run. I realized that I did not even know myself outside of being a runner. What did I like? What was I good at? What was important to me? I started to find myself after having lost myself years ago as a child.

After a few weeks of working the night shift at the gym, I decided I couldn't take the late hours and isolation, so I opted for a more traditional work schedule at an orthopedic practice. About halfway through the summer, I started walking to my new job. The trek was five miles through the city, but I realized it was the quiet time I craved by not running, plus, it was nice to see parts of the city I usually missed while taking public transportation. I continued walking to work through the end of the summer, and then progressed to running. I slowly started training again. Every morning I would run about 3 to 4 miles, and I was amazed at how quickly my endurance returned.

My body also seemed to naturally change much more effortlessly and rapidly. I lost body fat and overall weight without consciously trying and was running faster again. The break seemed to be exactly what I had needed to get my body and mind back into the sport. I eased back into racing, and although my times were not nearly as fast as they were in high school, they bettered my race times in college.

50.
"I was blarfing!"

IN THE BEGINNING OF 2009, I decided I wanted to try running a marathon. I had just raced in my first half marathon and loved it. The half marathon, although freezing, was a great experience and I finished in less than 90 minutes, which was my goal. In college, the maximum race distance is only ten kilometers (6.2 miles), and even though I never raced this event in college due to injuries, I had competed in a few 10k road races over my career as a younger runner. (My first one was in eighth grade with my sister Ashleigh. Neither of us had ever covered six miles during one run, and it was quite the mental and physical challenge!) I decided half marathons and marathons could be optimal race distances for me, because I have always been a runner who is more competitive at the longer distances. Even though I lack raw speed, I have excellent endurance.

I decided to train for Burlington's Vermont City Marathon that May. I chose this race because it seemed like a manageable number of weeks to train, I had always loved Vermont, it wouldn't be too hot yet, and most other marathons were already sold out. Since I didn't have any experience running twenty-six miles without stopping, I was nervous. The longest run I had ever completed was probably sixteen or seventeen miles. Even when I was severely anorexic, I never ran ridiculously far. A couple of times I got lost, and many times I ran multiple times per day, but I did not embark on long, continuous runs. Ten miles was a usual "long run" for me.

I started to read all about marathon training and plan my own training schedule. Each Sunday morning, I set out on solo long runs in Riverside Park and sometimes Central Park. There were several Sundays that winter that I certainly did not feel like running for two hours by myself, but I toughed it out, and did a very good job with my training. Ben, who was my fiancé by this time, was very supportive and always understood when I needed to lie down at home most of the day after a long run.

One of my difficulties in training for the marathon was a gastric ulcer I developed in my freshmen year of college from prescribed Ibuprofen. The sports medicine doctor put me on 800mg three times a day for eight to twelve weeks, for a stress fracture. Because this dosage came in a big white pill rather than four red tablets three times per day, I did not have a real appreciation of how much I was taking. Over time, I started to develop burning stomach pain when I would exercise after taking the pill, and since I was cross-training twice per day, this happened frequently. I decided to stop taking the medicine, but little did I know, the damage had already been done.

The ulcer was eventually treated, but I continue to suffer residual pain and cannot take any non-steroidal anti-inflammatories (NSAIDs). The long efforts during marathon training seemed to exacerbate the pain. There were numerous times I was doubled over on the couch when I got home, remaining in the fetal position until I fell asleep.

My longest training run before the marathon was roughly 21 miles. I did not run with fancy technical watches or distance calculators, so I never knew for sure, but I estimated distances by mapping the courses I ran online. Other than the first 10k road race I struggled through in eighth grade, I had never run a race before where I had not yet even completed the distance in training, so there was certainly a great deal of doubt and anxiety in my mind about completing the race.

The morning of the race was cool and rainy. As I sat with Ben and waited for the race to start, my body was stiff from the cold air. When the gun finally went off, I went out fast. The first several miles wound through hilly neighborhoods of Burlington. I was flying. Way too fast. There was not a race clock until mile five. This was problematic because the race had started late, and I had no idea how long I had been running. By the time I saw the clock, I realized how fast I was going, so I slowed down a notch. It was frankly a little late. The excitement of the race was pulling me along. I developed a side stitch at mile ten and struggled in the back hilly section. *Just hold it together, Am. You've run more than this hundreds of times.* I crossed the half marathon mark in a personal best time for me – not something that you want to have happen while running your first marathon, because you want to conserve your energy for the end of the race.

I struggled up the largest hill in the race, approaching the fifteen-mile mark, and saw Ben cheering for me. Earlier that morning, Ben and I devised a code so I could communicate how I was feeling if I wasn't able to run over and talk to him. I gave him a thumbs-down: this is not going well. The next eleven miles were pretty rough. Because I had a side stitch, it became very painful to breathe as I ran. I started walking, which was probably a mistake because I quickly saw how much more comfortable it was to walk rather than run.

I started stopping at each of the water stations to "refuel." I ate watermelon, orange slices, and even a whole soft pretzel. I walked and ran for a few miles, and then around mile twenty, I started feeling better, so I jogged the better part of the last six miles. As I finally entered the field where the finish was, I was overcome with emotion. *Twenty-six miles, only 0.2 to go!* But with the finish line in sight, I started vomiting continuously. Everything I had consumed en route was violently being shed from my body while I tried to sprint to the finish line. As I crossed the line, one of the medical staff personnel whisked me into the medical tent to recover. I started crying, "I need Ben. I want Ben!" When he was called, Ben came running in. Delirious from the run, I reported, "I was blarfing!"

When I was feeling better, Ben and I slowly walked back to the car and drove to our hotel in the neighboring town. I was sore, had a stomachache, and was very tired. In the shower, I started crying again. "I didn't get my medal!" Ben looked at me confused and said, "What?" I informed him that all finishers receive a medal, and I really had my heart set on it. "Why didn't you tell me when we were there, babe?" "I forgot." Being a good sport, Ben drove us back to the finish line where runners were still finishing, and explained to one of the volunteers that I had finished but didn't get to walk through the chute because I had gotten sick. She presented him with a medal. I smiled and cried yet again. "Thank you!" It was a day of way more tears than normal! Marathons really take it out of you.

The rest of the trip was fun. It was Memorial Day weekend, so we spent a few days in Burlington. We played bocce and had dinner with one of my best friends from college, went to a science museum, took a long walk along abandoned railroad tracks, and sat on the docks of Lake Champlain, watching sailboats. I was very proud that I'd finished third in my age group in a time of 3:19:20 – pretty solid for such a poorly executed race on a difficult course. It was an experience that taught me a lot about perseverance, pacing, and completing what I set out to do. There was something refreshingly fun about feeling like such a novice again in a sport I had been doing for twelve years.

51.
Five Boroughs

SOON AFTER WE RETURNED to New York City after my marathon debut in Vermont, I decided I wanted to run another one. My finish time in Burlington was fast enough to qualify for the New York City Marathon that November. I excitedly registered and set my sights on executing a smarter and faster race in my city.

In some ways, training for the New York City Marathon was more difficult for me than the training for Vermont, even though I already had the experience under my belt. I've always been a disciplined, adventurous winter runner, someone who runs outside year-round unless there is unbelievably bad weather. I'm talking below freezing temperatures with sleet falling from the sky, and a wind so fierce that trees are doubling over. You can bundle up in the winter. The hardest part is the footing, but if you choose where to run strategically, it's not too bad.

But summer running is tougher for me. I get overheated very easily and because I have cardiac issues due to my eating disorder, it can be dangerous for my heart. This made the long runs challenging, because many of them took place in the end of the summer. The novelty had also worn off. Whereas each long run I completed for the Vermont marathon constituted my furthest run to date, this was no longer the case for round two. Since I had already run a full marathon by the time I was training for New York, the long runs were just that: long runs. There was not as much to be proud about. I am very motivated by accomplishing goals and challenging myself, and even though I set goals, they were not as exciting to me, since I knew the runs should be doable. With that said, the training went fairly well and I managed to complete all my planned long runs. Because I was relying exclusively on a training schedule I developed myself, I felt in control of the outcome.

The New York City Marathon has an amazing expo. Literally a few hundred vendors set up tables in the Javits Center along the West Side Highway to sell running-related products or advertise races. All runners are required to go to the expo prior to marathon Sunday in order to pick up their numbers, timing chips, and race bags. Upon entering the Javits Center, I was speechless. In the main atrium, banners several stories high depicting runners at the marathon's start along the Verrazano Narrows Bridge hang down, and you feel like you've stepped into the race. There were enormous video screens showing clips from previous marathons. I got goose bumps. Even though I left right after picking up my number (6445), I was filled with inspiration and pride for taking part in an event so big, and with such a huge legacy.

My mom came down from Amherst the day before the race so she could watch me run. At the crack of dawn on the morning of the marathon, she drove me down to South Ferry, the southern tip of Manhattan. Runners are shuttled to the start of the race in Staten Island, either on early ferryboats or from buses that leave from two libraries in the city. Due to road closures, race organizers have to get all marathon runners to Staten Island several hours before the start of the race. I had a 5:30 a.m. ferry and it would have taken 45 minutes on the subway to get there, so my unfalteringly generous mom drove me to the ferry terminal.

It was a cold, rainy morning: your typical dark November dawn. We were quiet in the car and I stared into the lights of New Jersey across the Hudson River. When we arrived at South Ferry, Mom wished me luck and told me she'd see me on the course. I gathered my things and headed into the terminal alone. I missed her and started to cry. I looked back and she was still there, as if she knew I'd want one more goodbye. I ran back to the car. "You'll be great, honey," she said. I smiled and told her to look for me.

I felt more positive and excited as I got out of the cold and entered the ferry terminal. Luckily, event volunteers told me I could sit around in the terminal and wait for the 6:00 ferry, an option that I happily took. I was glad to do anything to stave off waiting around on the cold, wet ground in Staten Island.

The ferry ride takes roughly 25 minutes. We were herded onto shuttle buses that took us to the starting area. The New York City Marathon has so many entrants (about 40,000) that runners are divided into three separate color groups. These colors start in slightly different areas (two on the upper level of the Verrazano Narrows bridge and one underneath). I was green – local elite start. I walked to the green start camp, where people were stretching, resting, and using Port-a-potties. While I was waiting, I ate a light snack and drank some water. I was, without a doubt, lonely. Most other people seemed to have teammates or friends running with them. I sat on a trash bag and listened to my iPod, eager for the race to get underway. About an hour before the start, we checked our bags with the UPS truck that correlated with our race number, leaving behind our extra possessions and heading to the waiting pen. The smartest thing I packed was an extra pair of socks. The light drizzle and melting frost had saturated my socks, and with a fresh pair on, I felt warmer.

I was in the first wave; gun time was 9:40 a.m. It was a long, chilly, anxious hour before the race started, but I hit it off with a man in my pen that had traveled from New Zealand. He had previously raced the New York City Marathon and told me about the good parts and things to look out for. "People on the upper level of the bridge pee, so don't stand on the edge since we're underneath." Sound advice. His goal was 3:15. I told him I was on the same page. We talked about his life in New Zealand and mine in New York. About fifteen minutes before the start of the race, it was finally time to line up. I shed my extra layers of clothes (they get donated to the Salvation Army) and lined up in my corral. I was close to the starting line. Although the rain had stopped, my legs were cold. My feet were numb.

As usual, goose bumps covered my arms during the Star Spangled Banner. At the sound of the starting cannon, the New York City Marathon was underway. I started slow, which was good, as the course ascends over the bridge and then descends on the far side. My feet were so numb from being cold that I felt like I was hopping on potatoes rather than running fluidly. About two miles in, they finally thawed. By mile three, I got a slight side stitch, so I slowed down a little bit as a preventative measure. The side stitch was a dull annoyance, but I had learned from the Vermont Marathon that it could quickly escalate into something debilitating.

I listened to biochemistry audio lectures about the electron transport chain during the race. Music was too motivating for me, and I worried it would influence me to start out too fast. The lectures were enough of a distraction to help the time pass. My mom and Ben were cheering for me around the eight-mile mark in Brooklyn, but the streets were so crowded with runners and spectators, and I wasn't sure exactly where they were going to be. I missed them. However, the silver lining was that I kept looking for them through mile 9.5, at which point I realized I must have passed them. This hopeful search helped me through a few miles. Then I got in my groove. After mile ten, I was cruising. I was relaxed and pain-free and comfortable with my pace.

My favorite moment of the race was crossing the 59th Street Bridge that connects Queens to Manhattan. Entering Manhattan felt like I was coming home (even though you still have to leave again and go through the Bronx and back). The crowds were wild and empowering. I started loving every block as I ran up First Avenue toward the Bronx. My mom and Ben were going to be around mile 20, and I could feel myself closing in on them. Because spectators were sparse in the Bronx, it was far easier to spot them. Mom was standing up the course a little ways from Ben, so I saw her first. Initially, she did not see me because I was significantly ahead of my predicted time. I started waving wildly and smiling. "GO AM!" she screamed. I felt like a superstar. I cruised down the street and saw Ben. "I'm having so much fun!" I yelled. This time, I gave him the thumbs up.

The next few miles went pretty well as I returned to Manhattan and approached the finish line. I was flying along and felt so happy. The overwhelming feeling of exhaustion and heaviness known as "the wall" finally hit me around mile 24, but I knew I was almost done. The last two miles of the marathon course have some continuous, although slight, uphills. When I came to mile 25, I had about nine minutes to get to the finish (1.2 miles) in less than three hours. This was far more ambitious than my initial goal, but suddenly seemed attainable.

But the last half-mile crawled on. The race organizers delineate the final six hundred meters by one-hundred meter increments, and it felt like a minute per sign. I finally saw the finish and I mustered everything I could. The clock is not necessarily an accurate representation of your finish time, because in most large races you are usually positioned well behind the start line depending on your intended pace. The clock indicates "gun time." Runners are timed based on "chip time" – your time begins when you actually cross the start line.

I threw my hands in the air as I crossed the line and proudly walked through the chute. Even though I knew that I did not break three hours, because I had been very close to the start, I was still thrilled. Hundreds of volunteers lined the next half-mile of the park, handing out finish medals, aluminum blankets, and water. I saw my friend Nick from high school, who picked me up and whirled me around. "Great race!"

I started walking faster and faster, almost a jog, because I was so excited to find my mom and Ben at our pre-arranged meeting spot on Columbus Avenue. I was smiling and waving to all of the volunteers. When I finally got out of the park, I grabbed my checked bag from the UPS truck and trotted to Columbus Avenue. I saw them and started running into their arms. "I did it!" They were both impressed by how fast I had run.

I was rapidly getting cold, so we jumped in a cab and headed back to my apartment in Harlem. I went to the marathon's website and learned that I ran 3:01:02 – good for third in my age group again (although in a much more competitive race). I danced around the apartment. It was an unbelievably proud moment for me.

Since then, I have not run another marathon. I signed up to run Boston the following year, but injury prevented me from running. That setback, along with other injuries, the scheduling challenges of my job, and new training goals have kept me from running another one to date. Although, I hope that sometime in the next few years, I'll get back at it. You need to have a lot of time dedicated to training to execute a well-run marathon. I am also handicapped by an injury-riddled body from years of starvation and overtraining. That will always be my overwhelming obstacle from completing the intensely long training necessary for marathon success.

52.
"Childhood" Can Fit in Cardboard Boxes

MY PARENTS' DIVORCE WAS finalized in June 2010, and in November 2012, my mom finally sold our childhood house. The house I grew up in is a lot more than a four-bedroom, two-floor structure located at 85 Alpine Drive. It was my home for twenty-two years. February 1, 1991 was the day we moved in. I was four years old. My parents had picked out my bedroom – the smallest of the four. Although small, I liked it because it had two windows and a big closet.

On move-in day, my parents needed to keep me occupied while the movers brought our furniture into the correct rooms. They set up my plastic expandable toy tunnel in my bedroom. It was like a six-foot-long slinky that I could crawl through. I made it my fort and listened to the heavy footsteps of the moving guys trudging up and down the stairs with boxes. "It says bedroom. Put it here." "This one says fragile dining room. That goes back downstairs." The grunting and groaning from the movers frightened me. I rolled in my tunnel to my closet. I realized how fun rolling was, so I rolled back and forth in the tunnel until I would hit one wall, and then go back the other way. Eventually, I lay on my back and fell asleep.

Our house is where my sisters and I grew up. It's where I went from being a tiny little girl to a full-fledged adult. I loved running from our home. Situated in a nice wooded neighborhood called Echo Hill, my home base for running was great. I could run in all four directions, which allowed running to be more varied. From many houses, particularly ones located on major roads, you can really only go right or left. I could choose to run in the woods – just a two-minute jaunt from Amethyst Brook, a very large, wooded conservation area - or I could choose to do a hilly, secluded run, or even a flat run on populated roads.

One summer, I did almost 90 percent of my base mileage training for cross-country in Amethyst Brook. I would disappear there for an hour at a time, sheltered from the blazing heat of the sun by the canopy of trees. It kept me youthful while I ran - leaping over roots and rocks, scrambling up steep slopes. On the roads I have always had a tendency to put excessive pressure on myself, focusing too much on speed by comparing my time for the route to previous times on the same loop. So it was always a welcome break to run in Amethyst Brook, which distracted me from the stress I put on myself to attain goals on the pavement.

One reason the sale of my childhood home was so painful for me is because I feel like in many ways, I missed out on my childhood. I grew up too fast, consumed by a ravaging disease. Because my parents are now divorced, the home is the place where my memories of "family" live. It is the roof under which all five of us lived together. We were an extremely tight clan growing up; our deepest friendships were among ourselves. I miss the comfort of living with all of my best friends, and I am filled with regret and sadness about the strain that my eating disorder had on my relationship with my mom. Today, as she lives alone in a new house, I am saddened to have caused her disappointment. The notion that I was too much of a handful wears heavily on my conscience.

I visited home at the end of the summer for my wedding reception and at that point, the house was on the market. While my mind knew it was going to sell, the reality did not sink in. Sure, we were packing up my room and my mom had me sort through my old things, but it still felt like my house. I ate at the kitchen table. I slept in my childhood bed, looking out the same window I always did. When I put on my running shoes on the morning of our wedding reception I turned left and wound through my neighborhood and up to my favorite loop in the town of Pelham.

A few weeks after I had returned to New York from the wedding reception, my mom told me that she had found buyers and was closing the deal. There were boxes in the basement filled with my trophies, medals, and other accolades, as well as piles of newspaper clippings highlighting my race performances. Some boxes were labeled simply "Amber Running," others, "Amber Memories." When we were moving, I decided not to go through these boxes. I wasn't ready. They now sit in the basement of my in-laws' house. While my mom was immersed in the move and ready to get out, I never got to say goodbye. My oldest sister, Ashleigh, visited Amherst the final week that my parents owned 85 Alpine Drive. She said she walked around to each room and said goodbye. She texted me that day: "You'd be happy to know that my last memories of your room is being in there with mom and John [our family dog]. I said goodbye for you."

When I went home the following Thanksgiving, the house was no longer ours. I drove by and cried, longing to go in and see my old room one more time. I even got dropped off close to the house one morning to run a familiar loop. It was my best run of the week. I ran fast and felt good. Those runs may no longer be as easy for me to access, but my heart knows those streets will always be my stomping grounds.

53.
Differences Between my Anorexia and Textbook Cases

FROM WHAT I HAVE heard, read, and researched about eating disorders, it seems there are a few marked differences between my case of anorexia and the more textbook cases. I was younger than most people who develop an eating disorder. I made a conscious choice not to eat – not because I thought I was fat, but as I mentioned, to try to hold onto my childhood and somewhat ironically avoid the difficulties of being a teenager/adult (even though severe anorexia is a tremendous difficulty for any person), and to try to win over the affection and respect from my mom. These constitute extremely backwards thinking and couldn't have been more off the mark, but as a fifth grader, you don't always have the correct game plan given your limited experience in the world.

Similarly, by trying to stay thin and avoid growing up physically, I grew up faster emotionally than I ever could have imagined. I essentially gave up my childhood by the age of ten for a life of worrying, calculating, obsessing, and depression. I forfeited the "happiest girl in the world" persona, lost the ability to feel like people were taking care of me, and instead decided somehow I could do it better. I squandered the innocence that should be central in childhood – one that affords you days of imagination, play, fearlessness, and comfort. My anorexia eventually drove an enormous wedge between my mother and me, causing us to grow apart due to the incredible stress it placed on the parenting role and on our relationship. I felt isolated and "unloved" every time my parents yelled at me to eat—even though their passionate concern, I can see now, was clearly out of love.

A second difference is that I never wanted to weigh as little as I did. When I stepped on the scale, I wasn't hoping that it would show a smaller number than the week before. I literally covered my eyes and opened a slight gap between two fingers, squinting through in an attempt to obscure my view of the digital read-out, hoping it was higher than I imagined it would be. I didn't really care what the number was; I just wanted to be elite. As my disease progressed, once I started running, my determination to keep my body thin was solely because I thought it would allow me to be the most elite distance runner – my dream – and to me, it seemed no different than the body of my idols like Deena Kastor, Tegla Loroupe, or Paula Radcliffe.

I always had the restrictive type of anorexia – wherein caloric intake is controlled and limited, rather than the binge eating/purging type. While many anorexics cycle between various methods to remain thin, I never once took laxatives or diet pills, had enemas, or attempted to make myself throw up. But I certainly hated food, because it was the source of my agony and the thing that constantly put me "in trouble." I only ate to fuel my running. I ate the most in a day a few hours before the run, so that I would feel nourished and strong. I have always had a very sensitive stomach. I cannot eat immediately before exercising, or I get terrible side stitches. This meant that I had to eat enough calories three hours or so before practice so that I would not feel hungry for those three hours, as well as the two hours of practice.

This digestive difficulty probably saved me from literally starving myself to death. I was chasing my dreams of being a champion runner much harder than I was worried about caloric intake, and thus the running was paramount over anorexia. Had I not needed to fuel so robustly every day for my runs, perhaps I would have starved to death – a true paradox for an athlete in a sport that encourages athletes to be as thin as possible. What made me want to have extremely low body fat was the same thing that made me eat enough to survive. Perhaps if I was able to digest food like many runners, I could have had a small snack right before running and been sufficiently satisfied while eating even fewer calories per day, and would have become dangerously underweight even more rapidly. However, because eating before running would render the workout impossible for me, I had to eat several hundred calories in the early afternoon snack that kept my caloric intake up enough.

The severity of the illness flowed like a tidal pattern. It would flare up for several months at a time, then calm down before making its inevitable return. I was never completely out of the grasp of the disease during those years, but sometimes it was all that my life was, and other healthier times, only a part. It seemed to get progressively worse over the years, reaching peak severity the spring of my junior year of high school. But as a pattern, it was somewhat less of an issue the happier I was. It was a steady negative progression from its onset in fifth grade through the end of sixth grade.

Ironically, it got mildly better for a brief time during seventh grade, when I first took up running. During this time, I had a lot of novel things going on in a big, new school and was on a team where I made new friends. Eighth grade was much worse. I restricted more foods after realizing I was running faster the skinnier I became. I also hated eighth grade academically. I was extremely under-challenged in all of my classes and felt bored and detached. Freshman year, things improved because I was worried that I would not have enough energy to fuel me through the longer runs and races, as mileage was bumped up from middle school, so I ate a little more. My anorexia was at its worst during my sophomore and junior years. By that point, running fast was paramount and the thinner I became, the faster I got – a simple algorithm.

54.
Why Recovery is Difficult

ONE UNIQUE ASPECT OF eating disorders compared to other addictions is that everyone has to eat. If you are an alcoholic, your recovery requires that you stop drinking. If your addiction is gambling, illegal drug use, smoking, or even caffeine, these activities and substances can be avoided completely during and after recovery, so that the trigger is removed. Eating is a daily activity, often taking place at least three times per day. We must eat to remain alive. I believe this is the sole factor that makes eating disorders harder to overcome than other addictions. You are around the exact situation you want to avoid several times per day. It is always on your mind. In my opinion, this is why recovery rates are so low and recovery is so incredibly challenging. Food is simultaneously an unavoidable medicine, and a poison.

55.
"I don't have a problem."

A HALLMARK CHARACTERISTIC OF eating disorders is that people with the disease deny that they have a problem. Even after they have recovered, it is a topic they avoid. People don't want to come out and admit they had or have an eating disorder, because it is a source of shame – there is a stigma attached to the disease, like other addictions. Similar to a recovered alcoholic not wanting to discuss their former addiction, former anorexics both want to forget their past and separate themselves as far as they can from that part of their life. They do not want to lead on that they had a "problem" because it is embarrassing. This leads many people to remain silent on the subject.

The only way to know for sure that someone has an eating disorder is to receive a rare admission, or to view their physician's records. However, once you have lived as an anorexic, you build a familiarity so honed, you can tell without even knowing a person. Anorexia has a secret language that you learn over your years with the illness. By observing certain behaviors, I can be nearly positive whether someone does or doesn't have an eating disorder, as I am sure many other people who have had the disorder can do as well. This is more of a depressing truth than an ability I'm happy to have developed. Even after you confirm that someone does have a problem, there is virtually nothing you can do, leaving you feeling helpless as well as scared for the person you are concerned about.

56.

"For every action, there is an equal and opposite reaction"

HERE ARE A FEW FACTS about my growth and maturation. In sixth grade (age 11) I weighed 46 pounds, five pounds more than I did in the first grade (age six). Research indicates that between the ages of 6 and 10, children gain an average of 5 to 7 pounds per year.[9] That means I should have gained a minimum of 25 pounds. Five years later, I weighed only 70 pounds fully dressed with shoes on. What does this mean? Weight gain has two components – the increase in fat-free mass (muscle, bone, ligaments, etc.) and fat mass (adipose tissue). Both are important for maturation and development. Since I was deficient in both, this resulted in long-lasting consequences.

My adult height was stunted because I did not consume an adequate number of calories to promote growth. I have always been very short, even as a toddler, but I did not reach my potential height. When calorie intake is too low during puberty, the body must use all the energy coming in for immediate functions such as breathing, thinking, and digesting, rather than rebuilding, repairing, and growth. Once puberty is over, the body will no longer increase in height. Although everyone in my family is short, I am the shortest and robbed myself of probably a good three inches of height that I should have achieved, had I been eating a normal diet during puberty.

Numerous factors influence when a girl begins the onset of puberty that I feared so much. Some of these factors include genetics and other biological factors, environment, stress, and nutrition. Sufficient body fat must be present (medical professionals cite a range of 17 to 22 percent body fat). In the

United States, the average age of menarche (onset of menstrual periods) is 12.5 years old.[2] In my case, my mother as well as my sisters all began menstruation relatively early (10, 12, and 13), which theoretically should have predisposed me to a fairly early first period. However, due to my disease, this was not the case. The consequence of delayed menarche is loss of bone density, because the menstrual cycle is necessary for healthy bone development.

Furthermore, by not gaining an adequate amount of lean mass, my bones and muscles were very weak. This was compounded by the fact that I didn't get my first period until I was nineteen years old, at which point, the damage was already wrought on my bone density. My body had to "steal" calcium from the bones for daily routine functions (calcium is important in bone and teeth health, as well as necessary for heart and muscle contraction). My bones became so leeched of calcium that by the age of sixteen, my bone density scan showed I had severe osteopenia in my hips and wrists and nearly osteoporosis in my spine. The mineral density of my bones (an indication of their strength) was equated to that of an 82-year-old. Practically speaking, this meant my susceptibility to injury, particularly stress fractures, was very high.

Some of the most measureable damage was inflicted on my metabolism. When someone eats below their basal metabolic rate (BMR- the amount of calories they burn just by resting 24 hours in order to conduct normal bodily functions), the body perceives that it is starving. In my case, this was the daily norm for about eight years. The human urge to survive is the strongest instinct that we possess. When an individual is not consuming enough calories for everyday bodily functions, his or her body digests its own muscle. This occurs because muscle is more metabolically active (burns more calories) than fat tissue, which is also metabolically active, but to a much lesser degree. At rest, a pound of fat consumes about five calories in a day, whereas muscle burns through about fifteen. If your body can get rid of more muscle, it can subsist with fewer calories during starvation and still survive.

What this means for even the average dieter is that if calories are restricted too aggressively (below your BMR), there will be a measureable loss of lean body mass, rather than fat tissue. When adequate caloric intake resumes, the individual can no longer eat as many calories as would be expected for his or her body size without gaining weight, because of the reduced percentage of the most metabolically active tissue – muscle. This is often why yo-yo dieting occurs. If a person restricts his or her calories too much, he or she may regain all that weight, plus more (because his or her metabolism slowed due to loss of the muscle mass), making it even harder the next time weight loss is attempted. It is natural to think that you would lose fat first, but if caloric restriction is too drastic, you actually lose much more muscle than fat, which is not the goal of the majority of dieters. For an athlete, this phenomenon is extremely counterproductive. Not only does an athlete's performance depend on high-quality muscle, but body fat (which does not contribute to gains in athleticism) is desired to be low.

Even though I continued to run during my recovery, I gained weight incredibly fast. My body and metabolism refused to burn the calories you might expect for someone of my size and activity level, because it desperately clung to every calorie I consumed. My metabolic rate did not normalize until I was able to successfully put on a substantial amount of muscle mass through progressive resistance training. Not surprisingly, this took a very long time. Even male body builders, whose job it is to put on lean muscle mass, are lucky if they put on 7 to 10 pounds of muscle in a year – and that is often with the "help" of ergogenic aids. Women have an even harder time gaining muscle mass than men due to substantially lower levels of testosterone, the hormone that plays a pivotal role in increasing muscle mass. Despite the common fear among women that they will "bulk up" due to resistance training, it is very difficult for women to gain substantial muscle mass.

After I finally began the recovery process, I struggled with a very slow metabolism for the next seven years. Over 2,500 days of trying to repair your metabolism feels like an eternity when you are going through it. I had a very large weight rebound (gained more weight than I needed to). This was partly due to the fact that I was severely overeating and because I had destroyed my metabolic rate. It took several years, a disciplined diet at times, painstaking patience, and emotional turmoil to get my weight on the right track and achieve a healthy body composition.

Muscle loss as a result of starvation does not just occur in skeletal muscle. The digestive tract is lined with smooth muscle, and we have cardiac muscle (the heart), arguably the most important organ for a runner. I caused severe damage to my heart because my body was literally digesting my heart muscle, while distance running was putting incredible demands on my cardiovascular system. Simultaneously, my malnourished state resulted in severe electrolyte imbalances that affected my heart. Proper electrolyte proportions are required to maintain healthy heart contractions. I caused permanent damage that still disturbs my heart today. My heart had always been very healthy. Endurance exercise is wonderful for building a strong heart and cardiovascular system. However, with the severe caloric restriction and over-exercising that escalated as my anorexia worsened, the demands on my heart were too taxing.

One summer afternoon at the end of high school, I was running in Amethyst Brook. My heartbeat was noticeably off. I wasn't able to pinpoint what the issue was, but I was aware that it felt strange. As the run progressed, I knew I needed to stop. I ran home and couldn't even make it inside the front door before I collapsed in the driveway. Luckily, my mom was home and heard the family dog, John, barking excitedly upon my arrival. The good watchdog. Mom came outside after a few minutes when I hadn't come in. She called the ambulance, and we were swept to Cooley Dickinson Hospital. The emergency room physicians explained that my EKG revealed abnormalities – my heart was not functioning properly. I was rehydrated with lots of fluid and proper electrolytes. Thankfully, my cardiac rhythm normalized. I was lucky that I was young and otherwise relatively healthy.

Sodium, potassium, and calcium are three important electrolytes involved in muscle contraction. The heart needs certain ratios and absolute concentrations of these electrolytes to contract properly. My body was so deficient in electrolytes that these contractions were not normal. Unfortunately, I still have permanent heart arrhythmias due to the damage I caused to my heart tissue, as well as its electrical conductivity system. Despite many trips to various cardiologists, no treatment currently exists. I am left to try and reduce the likelihood of a fatal cardiac episode by making sure I am always adequately hydrated and have electrolyte replacements, especially when I sweat a lot. There was also a time after the initial diagnosis of this arrhythmia condition where cardiologists prohibited me to get my heart rate during training over 150bpm. This resulted in very slow, easy jogs, and yet another frustrating example of missed training.

My reproductive system also sustained long-term physical damage as a result of my eating disorder. Although I pretended I had periods when I was younger (I think 17) because I wanted doctors to get off my back, I was three weeks from turning nineteen when I finally got my first period. My delayed menarche further exacerbated my bone loss because estrogen is essential in healthy bone maintenance. I still have abnormal and erratic periods; my gynecologist has informed me that I may never be able to bear children. A twelve-, fourteen-, or even seventeen-year old doesn't really care about that, but now that I am twenty-six and married, it's something both my husband and I will have to face.

When you combine all the aforementioned factors, it's clear to see why my running took a substantial hit as I recovered from anorexia. Principally speaking, I was much heavier and carried a disproportionately large amount of body fat (compared to lean mass) because I had lost so much muscle mass, and it is very hard to gain this tissue back. My bones, muscles, tendons, and ligaments were only accustomed to carrying about 70 pounds, and because my weight increased by 50 percent in one year, these structures and tissues didn't get the chance to build up gradually, like they would have if I had gone through a more natural puberty.

Relatively speaking, I put on lots of weight suddenly, and most of it was fat, so physiologically, it was basically like I was wearing a weighted vest. It was incredibly difficult to run fast because my body was too weak for my new weight. As a result, injuries occurred like falling dominos, my bones literally crumbling because they were so frail. I spent very few consecutive weeks running at one time before another injury would strike, and I would be confined to some non-weight-bearing cross-training apparatus for three or four months. You don't become a good runner on a stationary bike or pedaling an elliptical. As I mentioned, my heart was damaged so I could not train intensely, and to this day, I still have to remain careful.

The longest lasting and hardest consequence to bear was not physical. It was the damage to my relationships, particularly with my mom. My anorexia caused us to fight constantly, putting tremendous strain and stress on our relationship. It pushed a wedge between us, and eventually we became virtually estranged. This pales in comparison to the fact that I lost her trust. Years of lying about what had and hadn't been eaten, where I had been at various times, how much I had run, and my overall "shady" behavior did not lend itself to maintaining anyone's trust. It took several years and the compassion that pretty much only a mother can possess for our relationship to be repaired, and for me to prove that I deserved her trust again.

Because I had lost her trust, I also struggled to gain her respect as I pulled out of the disease. She challenged many of my decisions, and we often found ourselves at odds with one another. I believe she still viewed me as a little kid because I had not really gone through puberty physically or emotionally, and this made it unnatural for her to let me make my own choices toward the end of high school and through college. It was as if she still felt I needed to be parented through everything, and that made me extremely angry. I did not want to be told what to do. I was already an "adult" at eighteen. Over time, we rediscovered how to communicate with one another, which began the long, slow process of mending our relationship.

To this end, it also took me a while to understand that my mom loved me, and that it was precisely because of this love that she was always on my case about eating. During the years that my eating disorder was at its worst, it just seemed like she wanted to strangle me. I thought I was nothing but a problem she had to fix.

I also lost many friends during those years. It was not that I was directly lying to them, but I didn't want to hang out with anyone socially, and no one really wanted to hang out with me in return. Friends asked me to hang out, but I blew them off. I was worried the restaurants they wanted to go to would have too much food, or people would notice I wasn't eating at a slumber party, or I had planned to run that afternoon and if I went over to their house, I'd miss a valuable training session. There were always excuses in my mind and "good reasons" to not go. Over time, people stopped inviting me to things. Who would continue to try to include me if I never accepted an invitation?

For a long while it didn't bother me, because I wanted to be alone, but once I started trying to recover, I needed a wide support system. But I had a barebones assembly of a couple of people I had kept in my life. Because I had isolated myself during the depths of the disease, I had lost most of my valuable relationships. As I gained weight, I felt like a fat ogre, clomping through the halls of my high school, people pointing and laughing, whispering to one another about how I used to be fast. I felt embarrassed in my own skin and ashamed to bring up or admit that I had an eating disorder and try to make amends.

I still know many of those people today, and they are all beautifully kind individuals. I am confident that nearly all of them would have accepted my apology and would have been there to support me, but I was too ashamed and too introverted to reach out and ask for help in my recovery, or even for just the simplicity of their friendship. Long term, I also missed out on years of developing communication and social skills during adolescence. Much of my young adult life has been peppered with the realization that these skills are some of my weakest areas and are the most important for relationships of all types – in the family, dating, friendships, and business.

In that vein, I completely lost my own self-respect. Once I finally woke up and started trying to fight back against the disease, I saw the person I was left with, and I was ashamed of her. I had lost friends, hurt my family through years of stress, lied to people I loved, defined my self-worth by my race performances, and felt like I was worth nothing. I felt like a loser, someone without values, and someone who didn't deserve to be loved or to be happy. What's more, for the previous eight years, I had defined my value by being a great runner. *Who's Amber? She's a super-fast runner.* Nothing about my personality, nothing about my other interests. My identity was my sport. As I gained back the weight that my body needed, my running suffered terribly. This made me feel absolutely worthless, because if I was not fast, I had nothing except the memories of being fast. I had no idea who I was as a person outside of the sport.

One of the hallmarks of eating disorders is a distorted body image. Mine was very distorted, and frankly still is to a lesser degree. Even in my thinnest days, I knew I was very skinny, but in my eyes, I usually looked healthy. I looked fast. I looked like a superstar runner. In hindsight (and by looking at photos of myself), I was much skinnier than "superstar runners." I looked sick. In fact, it's actually quite emotionally painful for me to look at old photos of myself, partially because I remember what I went through, and partially because I look so emaciated.

Even now when I stand in front of the mirror naked, I don't usually like what I see. It is my understanding that most women hate certain parts of their bodies, have "fat" days, and are overly critical, but I think I see my whole body as fatter than it actually is. Because I grew into my short adult height when I was sickeningly thin, I feel stocky with normal weight on my petite frame. People tell me I am not, but that doesn't change the fact that I feel heavy – not necessarily "fat," just "big," like I take up a lot of room.

While it's sad that this is still an issue for me, this distortion has lessened over the last couple of years, whereas it was a pretty major issue for the six years or so after I began to recover. In some of those darker days, I felt so incredibly ugly. I felt like a ball of hideous, blubbery jelly. I'd look down at my body and couldn't believe it was myself. I would hide my figure under loose sweatshirts and big, baggy jeans. The purpose was two-fold – it made me feel smaller and hid my "disgusting" body. I continued to isolate myself because I worried that people would make fun of me to my face or behind my back if I went out. I stopped dating and stopped hoping to make friends. I thought I didn't deserve relationships anyway.

This led to incredible loneliness in college. Both at Duke and UMass, I struggled to have any inkling of a social life. Later in my tenure at UMass, I had some friends, but my relationships were largely superficial and I always felt like an outsider. On the buses to meets, I always sat by myself – not because I wanted to, but because it seemed like no one wanted to ride with me. When you don't hold yourself in a confident manner, you are not attractive to others. I did not seem approachable and made very little effort to change that.

It was a cyclical problem: I was very depressed because I hated my body, felt useless and like a failure, and therefore had no friends because I stuck to myself, and because I had no friends, I became more depressed. This depression was magnified by family problems that were separate from my own issues. Eventually I became suicidal, but was heavily treated with antidepressants and therapy three days a week. The new therapist, unlike the one I had growing up, was a woman who I greatly respected. If nothing else, the fact that she made me come three times a week made me feel like someone cared that I stuck around.

My eating disorder robbed me of my childhood because I was preoccupied from fifth grade through high school. I missed out on growing up, enjoying carefree days of youth, and just being a kid. There is a big hole in my heart, an ache to relive those days. Even as a young child, I was both mature and immature at the same time. I have severe ADHD, which has often caused me to be extremely silly, hyperactive, and unable to control myself in the way that my peers could.

As a kid, I enjoyed childish things longer than my peers did. I liked playing with dolls, board games, playing outside in the yard, and creating make-believe games, even by myself. At the same time, I was mature in many aspects as a child. I was very bright, liked helping other people, conversed well with adults, and was empathetic toward others markedly more than most people (to the point that I cry when I see someone I know cry, because it is painful for me to see them sad). The fact that my personality landed on both sides of the spectrum of childish and adult behavior meant that I often found myself in a sort of no-man's land when it came to making friends.

57.
Celiac

I HAVE CURRENT DIETARY restrictions, although no longer by choice or due to mental illness. In the beginning of 2012, I was diagnosed with celiac disease. Celiac disease is an autoimmune disorder wherein if gluten (the protein in wheat and other grains) is consumed, the body starts attacking its own healthy cells.

Celiac disease has a large genetic component, but those with celiac are over ten times more likely to have another autoimmune disease or food allergies. While numerous case studies have looked at the link between eating disorders and celiac disease, there have not been sufficient large-scale studies to draw conclusions. This is probably because there are relatively few people with the celiac diagnosis, and current and former anorexics are unlikely to step forward due to the disease's stigma. Celiac is a genetic disease I was born with, but it often does not start affecting the individual until some sort of traumatic event, life change, or illness. Cause and effect still remain unclear, and therefore my doctors inform me that they cannot definitively say that my prolonged anorexia caused celiac disease, but it might have been the factor that triggered the disease to affect me.

My body also cannot properly digest and absorb dietary fats. I ate very little fat growing up, and virtually none during eight years of anorexia. As a result, my gall bladder does not effectively secrete bile, which the body needs to break down fat molecules.

While removing gluten from my diet initially alleviated my celiac disease symptoms, several months later, digestive issues returned. In late 2012, an immunologist determined I am allergic to dairy, yeast, soy, egg, and shellfish as well as intolerant to corn and several varieties of nuts. Additional food allergies are not uncommon for individuals with celiac disease, but trying to piece together a nutritious diet with so many restrictions certainly presents a challenge. Additionally, dining out in a restaurant is virtually impossible, which gets frustrating and presents challenges when trying to maintain a social life.

58.
Friends Forever

AS I MENTIONED, I re-met Samantha the first day of seventh grade cross-country, after knowing of her through our mutual childhood friend, Brooke. Samantha and I learned that we were on the same "team" in middle school (our organizational structure for dividing students in classes). We instantly bonded. Our personalities clicked and we became good friends, "the duo," so to speak.

Samantha blossomed in college; I struggled. I had too much pride to always be totally honest about how unhappy I was, although I did let on to it, particularly through Duke and my transfer to UMass. We rarely talked about serious things, although I'm not sure exactly how we fell into that pattern. Our relationship, while close in some ways, was also shallow. We never once talked about my eating disorder. We talked about what all friends talk about – school, practice, the team, our families, boys, other friends, goals, fears, and the like. I felt safe around her because she never made me feel weird in terms of my personality (even though I'm a bit of an odd-ball) or physically (because I was so skinny) or even behaviorally regarding the eating disorder.

Samantha and I dubbed ourselves "partners in crime." Her enthusiasm for the sport matched mine. Even though our running abilities were very different, we both truly supported one another and enjoyed the process to the same degree. I respected her determination and her passion for running, and loved her as a person. We were undoubtedly best friends. Even after we graduated high school, we remained good friends, although our communication became much more sporadic and we only managed to see one another on major holiday vacations.

Our relationship started to suffer during our first years at college. Samantha was not affected emotionally by our significantly reduced communication. When we were able to spend time together during holidays at home in Amherst, Samantha could simply pick up where we left off. That was not the case for me; I missed talking so frequently and sharing so many experiences together. As Samantha began to thrive and love school during her first year in college, I was miserable at Duke and felt like we were growing apart, because our experiences were so different.

Honestly, I was not jealous that she was happy. In fact, I loved her so much that I was happy for her – it just made me feel alone in my misery and like I was weird to be hating school. I struggled terribly to make friends at Duke because everyone seemed so different than me, and I secluded myself as I became more depressed. I really needed my old high school friends like Samantha, while she had tons of new friends and did not have the "need" for me. Being the bad communicator that I was, as well as protecting my ego, instead of being honest with her that I desperately needed her, I pretended I was fine.

Even so, I was still under the impression that Samantha valued our friendship more than her other ones, including her college relationships. In high school we were the best of best friends, and since I had not replaced her in any way, it was foreign to me that having newer, better, or at least more relevant friendships was a possibility. To me, she was still my best friend, because I had been unable to form deep friendships with my teammates or classmates at Duke, UMass, or even in New York. I had a handful of other close friends, but Samantha was basically right on top, even five years after high school. I simply became her high school best friend, but she had more meaningful pertinent relationships with others she had since met. We continued to communicate through email and see one another occasionally when we were home, but our relationship was weakening.

In early September 2011, I called our mutual friend, Chel, who also lived in New York City to see if she wanted to travel together to Samantha's wedding the next month. Chel informed me that she was one of Samantha's bridesmaids, so she would be going down a few days before the wedding. The news stung me. I was hurt - hurt that Samantha had chosen our other friend as a bridesmaid and not me, and hurt that Samantha didn't tell me herself. It was embarrassing to hear it from someone else, who assumed I was also a bridesmaid. It really made me realize how much she had moved on from the importance of our relationship, yet I had not. It was also painful to hear that another high school friend had been chosen over me since we were both friends from the same time in her life, and I had believed our friendship was more important. I had always imagined that Samantha and I would each play a central role in one another's wedding.

I was walking south on Saint Nicholas Avenue in Harlem when I made that call to Chel. I was heading to Modell's Sporting Goods, but the news hit me like a ton of bricks thrown one after another to my gut. I sat on a bench, crying and texting Ben through blurry eyes. He told me I was the best friend I could have been, and that it was a bad choice on her part.

I believe he was trying to help me feel better, and while there was probably some truth to what he was saying, a truer statement would have been: you were the best friend you could be, given your handicap of the disease. During the disease, I was preoccupied with my issues too much of the time to be a good friend. During recovery, I was too depressed, withdrawn from social life, and too weak to ask for her help. I had distanced myself too much, and we drifted apart.

I didn't go to Samantha's wedding. She was my best friend growing up, and I chose not to go to her wedding. Sure, I had a valid excuse - a commitment that weekend for continuing education conference for my career - but I could have missed that. I chose to not attend her wedding. I wasn't mature enough or emotionally strong enough at that point in my life to be there with the hurt I felt, and for that I feel weak and ashamed.

I regret that I did not attend, but regrets get me nowhere. I can only hope that someday, Samantha will be able to forgive me, let me back in to apologize, and we can move forward. About a month after her wedding, Samantha sent me an email and asked me never to contact her again; she was no longer interested in being friends. Reading the email felt like swallowing razor blades. No one had ever told me that we were no longer friends, and it made me realize how little I had been there for her when I was too wrapped up in my own world to even realize it.

The loss of her friendship was one of the most difficult repercussions of my anorexia. As I write this, we are no longer on speaking terms and haven't been since the end of 2011 – at her request. As I went through all my things at my mom's house from my adolescence while she prepared to sell the home, I was unable to ignore the enormous presence Samantha had in my life during those years. I had so many notes from her, motivational signs we crafted for one another, photos from races we attended together, mix CDs, and even a quilt she made. I was filled with a cold, empty feeling as I recalled the warmth, laughs, and companionship she provided for me while we were growing up. I had made it nearly a year without contacting her, as per her request. I caved and sent her a letter in the mail:

Hi Samantha,

It's okay if you don't want to read this. You can throw it away right now...or perhaps you didn't even open it. I understand why you would have done that. I hope though (and that's all I can do) that you will read it. I don't need you to respond, and I am trying to respect your request to never hear from me again so I let a lot of time pass and then tried to contact you in the least-invasive way that I could. I understand that you no longer want to be friends – I promise I'm not dumb, I am not trying to ignore your request, I just wanted a chance to say a few things because it would be unhealthy not to.

All I want to say is that you're right - you deserve a better friend. I'm a shitty friend. I'm not a bad person but I am not good at being social and I'm not who you deserve as a friend. You are absolutely correct that we are all too busy for someone who doesn't seem to put any effort back into a relationship. I know now that you don't want to be friends with me anymore so I am not going to bother you and explain what had been going on with me over the past several years - I don't want to disrespect your time. I only want you to know that I truly will always care about you and speak highly of our time together when we were young. For my own selfish sake, I wish I hadn't have been having certain problems and been a better friend because I know you would have been someone I'd love to be friends with for life - someone who'd be like an aunt to my kids someday. But this isn't about me; I already know I wasn't a good friend, why I sucked, and what I lost.

I just wanted to say that you'll always have an extra person in the world hoping for the best for you, thinking of you, and hoping some day if the world does me a favor, I'll be able to see you and help you in some anonymous way like a real friend and you won't have to deal with me but will somehow get the magic and it will just be the surface of what you deserve. You will always be someone who helped shape me - because that's what childhood and adolescence are about - and even though I understand that my actions to you over the past several years have demonstrated that I'm a shithead friend, if you ever need an extra friend to lean on, my door will always, always be open for you and hoping that peace will come so I can explain and give you what you deserve as the beautiful, smart, caring, friend that you are.

Take care,
Amber

I mailed that letter to her just after my 26th birthday - the first birthday since I turned twelve that I did not hear from her. The letter did not, and still has not, elicited any sort of response. A week after I sent it, I got married in a small family-only ceremony in our neighborhood in New York City. As I was getting ready, I thought about Samantha, remembering when we used to take walks in the woods by my house, wondering what kissing a boy would be like, trying to envision ourselves married one day, and imagining growing old as close friends in one another's lives. On her birthday a few months later, I could not contact her again. Her lack of response to my letter reinforced that she wanted nothing to do with me anymore. I thought about her for the majority of my wedding day, simply hoping she was doing well, imagining the hug I would give her if she walked through the ornate stonewall surrounding the park where Ben and I were married.

59.
Your Anorexia Stresses Me Out

EVER SINCE I BEGAN recovering from anorexia, it has been difficult for me to be around people with disordered eating. Unfortunately, it's a commonality among the women in my family. Just as some families have the same eyes, freckled skin, or bad teeth, Sayer women have eating issues. Ashleigh in particular has really struggled with an eating disorder, but not until well after college. My mom tends to vacillate between eating very little (her norm) to eating next to nothing. During these times, it can be a very trying situation for me.

A couple of years ago, my mom and I took a trip to Ashville, NC. It was the first trip that we had been on, just the two of us, since the trips we had taken together to go to National events in high school. I was shocked at how much her lack of eating made me feel pressured to eat less. It was impossible for me to separate myself from my mom's issues. During nearly every "meal" (I use that term loosely, because my mom really did not eat enough food to constitute a meal), I could not control my instinct to look over and compare the few bites of something light that she was having to what I was planning to eat. A constant inner battle went on in my mind. *Don't eat that granola bar; Mom's not having anything.* Or, after a long five-hour hike when she would have her apple for lunch: *You should be able to be satiated with just an apple as well. Why are you having all these other foods?*

I am not going to deny that part of me is jealous she can still be so disciplined in her dietary restriction. Despite hours of exercise, my mom eats probably less than 1,000 calories a day – I've never done the math, but it could be much less than even that some days. While I cannot say for certain that I am in fact jealous, because I have not been able to pinpoint that being one of the emotions that gets stirred up, it seems like a logical guess.

Lastly, and perhaps most true as I mature and my parents are now divorced, I worry tremendously about my mom. She is incredibly frail, and because she has eaten next to nothing for years, she doesn't have an ounce of body fat to spare. What happens if she gets sick and needs to be hospitalized? Her body doesn't carry an extra ounce of weight or an energy deposit to sustain her life. I love her so much and hope that she can find a way to overcome her challenges with eating enough food to be healthy.

60.
Working in the Fitness Industry

I DABBLED IN PERSONAL training while living in Amherst and attending UMass as an undergraduate student. I worked very short stints at nearly every gym within a fifteen-mile radius, but none of them could hold my attention. There is a popular misconception that being a personal trainer is easy. It is far from that, and while I was great at prescribing exercise, teaching clients, and planning appropriate workouts, I was awful at sales. In order to get paid as a trainer, you have to sell packages. On top of that, the trainer usually receives only a small percentage of the package price, and the gym takes the rest. A trainer must book many sessions per week to make ends meet. Sometimes gyms even require the trainer to maintain a certain amount of sessions per week, or he or she is let go, even though the gym only pays the trainer when they are working with someone anyway.

When the trainer is not working with a client, his or her job is to "work the floors." This involves pacing around eyeing individuals that look like they can afford a trainer, look like they need a trainer, and look like they would want what training services provide them. Then, the trainer has to approach the individual, try to demonstrate or teach them a tip on the spot, and give an elevator pitch about why they would benefit from a trainer, and why he or she is specifically a good match for them.

I have always been shy, lack self-esteem, and do not like to ask people for money. This is essentially the trinity of death for a personal trainer. You have to be incredibly outgoing, confident, fairly pushy, and sometimes downright deceptive. Particularly while I was in college, this was not the right environment for me, because I was consumed by severe depression. In fact, it contributed to exacerbating my depression because as I did not get clients, I felt less worthy, and more of a failure. I decided to quit trying to make it as a trainer and began to work exclusively at Hastings until I graduated.

When I moved to New York City, personal training was my only real marketable trade. It was my best bet for getting a job, and since I wanted so badly to escape Amherst, I was willing to jump back into it. By this time, I had earned my BS in Kinesiology, had more confidence in my abilities as an exercise professional, and had the added pressure of needing a job to afford to live in an expensive city.

With all this said, if I thought the fitness industry was tough in Amherst, I was in for a real shock when I moved to New York. On paper, I looked great. In fact, I got six jobs before I even moved down to the city (in one whirlwind day, I drove down with my mom, navigated through busy, unfamiliar streets, interviewed in six places, and was offered each one). In the city, personal training is a whole different animal. There are literally thousands of trainers – some are very educated, some are simply meatheads with or without certification. Some are great, while some could have you injured within five minutes.

Sex sells above all else in the world of New York City personal trainers. If you look hot and you know how to work it, you will be booked solid, regardless of your experience and education. First of all, I have never considered myself hot. Clearly someone with a severe eating disorder does not feel attractive, and as I gained weight, I felt like a short, fat, ugly horse.

I do not have a voluptuous, curvy body or a long and lean one. I am far from a tall, made-up flirty girl with long, blown-out blond hair, audacious jewelry, a cleavage-popping camisole and booty shorts. My tomboy-ish look pales in comparison. I do not usually wear makeup; I prefer the natural look. I'm an athletic brunette, usually sporting a ponytail and ill-fitting clothing. That's just the appearance end of things; there are also stark personality mismatches. The successful New York City female trainer knows how to walk the walk almost as well as a runway model. You have to flirt, show off your body in an alluring, yet subtle way, and convince clients that if they hire you, they will either look like you (if they are a woman) or get girls that look like you (if you are a man).

After a week at one job, I took a position at a different gym that seemed more promising because it had a base salary (albeit a low one) with commissions on top of that. All of the other jobs I had applied for were entirely commissions-based: you got paid if and only if you were working with a client. The new job was at a residential gym in a swanky, high-rise condominium building in Times Square. While clientele were wealthy, when it came down to it, there were hardly any patrons of the gym. One of the major downsides to working in a residential gym is that the client base is limited to people who live in the building. Some buildings have many empty units, and in some buildings, such as the one I worked in, the units that were occupied did not have many residents that frequented the gym.

The majority of the people I met from the building traveled extensively. One gentleman was a diamond seller, so he was constantly traveling abroad to buy and sell diamonds. Another man worked in Los Angeles and simply owned the unit in New York for when he wanted to visit. These two cases were not unique; they were the norm. With busy travel schedules, residents are around less frequently, further reducing the likelihood that they even check out the gym. Furthermore, in New York City there are dozens of exclusive, high-end fitness facilities. People that can afford to live in the building I worked in are typically the type of person who does not mind shelling out more money for the best exercise experience in town, even if they have a great one just an elevator ride away.

On top of this snag, I worked the night shift: 3:00 p.m. to midnight. This schedule proved to be socially isolating because I was working when my friends were free to hang out, and during the morning hours that I had off, I was the only one around not working. Another stressor was that when I left work after my shift and got off the train in my Harlem neighborhood just before 1:00

a.m., the streets felt unsafe. I would exit the subway station, clutch my bag to my chest, and run home, looking over my shoulder every block to make sure no one was following me. Once I had reached my front steps, the winter air had chilled my fingers and I'd struggle with my key in the door, sometimes dodging comments from homeless guys that slept on the church steps next door. *Just get inside, Am.*

Inside, I'd climb up the two flights of stairs and enter my silent apartment, my eccentric Craigslist roommates fast asleep. Sometimes I would eat, other times I would go right to sleep, but most nights I would lie awake on my uneven mattress, staring into the empty darkness of my room. *There's got to be more than this.*

About six weeks into this gig, I decided it was not working for me. I was not booking enough sessions, the one client I had told me I was "far too fat to be a trainer," and I lived a life of solitude on a different side of the clock than the people I wanted to spend time with. I ended up taking a receptionist position at an orthopedic practice in a hospital on the Upper East Side. I felt lucky to land the job, never having worked in an office before, and liked the regular 9-5 schedule it provided. This job turned out to be a wonderful opportunity for me, and I eventually moved up to be the surgical coordinator for one of the surgeons. Because it was a sports medicine practice, I was still somewhat involved in the field I was interested in, and as I had long wanted to be a doctor. It was the closest experience I ever had to being one. The surgeon I worked for was a very kind man and an enthusiastic runner. Sometimes after work we would run in Central Park – a long, slow run ending well past sunset.

After about a year, I missed being in school, learning, and being involved more directly in the field of exercise. I decided I wanted to go back to school for a Masters Degree in Exercise Physiology. I applied to Queens College and was accepted for Fall 2009. I continued to work as I pursued my graduate degree, taking five classes my first semester.

My final semester, the fall of 2010, I had to do a 150-hour internship in the fitness field. This was infuriating to me. I had already worked in the fitness industry in New York City, and it's hard to have the time and money to give away 150 hours of free labor. I went on eight or nine site visits: traveling to prospective internship positions, meeting with the directors and assessing whether the location would be a good fit for me. The last one proved to be the best fit for two reasons – it was about a six-minute walk from my apartment (and I've always hated wasting time commuting, plus I liked the idea of helping people from my neighborhood) and the man who owned the place was unbelievably sweet.

The internship placement was at a small studio called ARC Athletics, owned and operated by Gene Schafer. It was basically a personal fitness training studio with some additional clients coming in for sports rehabilitation programs, rather than strict fitness. It turned out to be the stimulus that would get me back into training clients. Long after my 150 hours were over, I voluntarily put in several hundred additional unpaid hours because ARC Athletics grew to be a place I loved: the first professional fitness environment that I truly thrived in.

Gene did not require me to book clients. Because ARC Athletics is a fitness studio rather than a gym, Gene does not need to do personal training sales in the traditional sense. Clients come to him; he doesn't troll the floor trying to get them. People cannot work out there unless they are already working with him (or me, at the time). I discovered that when I did not have to sell myself to get a client, but already had one, I was an incredible trainer. Clients listened to me, improved rapidly under my guidance, enjoyed their workouts, and requested to work with me. Moreover, although I experience a great deal of social anxiety, after some initial anxiety before their first session, I usually found it easy enough to talk to all my clients. While I was flourishing at the internship, I was flying through Queens College with blazing colors; in fact, I got a perfect 4.0 for my degree (which was very different than my undergraduate GPA) and finished in just three semesters.

Eventually I outgrew working for Gene and decided to embark on my own. Working for myself is exponentially more satisfying, because I have a choice about who I train and exactly what exercise program I develop based on the individual's goals and preferences. I also began an online certificate program from the Institute of Integrative Nutrition, which taught me hundreds of dietary theories, skills for coaching individuals with various health goals, and nutrition therapy for different diseases, as well as how to establish and operate my own business. The business curriculum greatly helped me build enough knowledge and confidence to take the leap out of Gene's safety net into my own venture.

Ultimately, I would like to have a greater impact in the health and fitness field. I want to be the impetus for major change in my clients' lives. I would love to be more involved in eating disorder education and prevention in athletes, particularly females. My heart aches knowing about all the girls who are suffering with this dangerous disease, and who are going to have to live with the after-effects for the rest of their lives, just as I have. Due to the nature of the mental disease and the fact that most people with eating disorders will not admit even to themselves that they have a problem, I think prevention is more effective than treatment. In fact, a study published by the National Association of Anorexia Nervosa and Associated Disorders found that only 30 to 40 percent of people with anorexia ever recover from the disease.

I know how vicious anorexia can be, and how dangerous it is that it can lead to short-term success for long distance runners. For females in particular, anorexia has the very unfortunate benefit of improving athletic performance, giving positive reinforcement for a negative behavior. Adding to this, many of the best distance runners are somewhat neurotic, type-A personalities. Distance running requires discipline. Come rain, snow, or fatigue – a runner has to push through. The best runners are often calculating people with the mindset that you can and should give more than 100 percent to be the best. It is exactly the same mindset many of the best distance runners embody that can lead to anorexia, and many people with anorexia possess similar personality traits as elite distance runners. They tend to be perfectionists, require organization and control, and calculate everything. Both groups tend to excel in academics, because it is also an environment where discipline and perfectionism pay off.

How does a distance runner develop an eating disorder? I believe, largely, through observation and experimentation. Runners want to be their best; they are constantly striving to improve – beating the clock, running further than ever before, and running faster. They calculate miles, memorize their race splits and best times, and think about how to improve. The "whatever it takes" mentality is paramount in the best runners. They don't allow weather, fatigue, pain, or fear to hold them back.

Because her personality drives her to want to be the best, the successful female runner looks around at who is still beating her, and at who the world-class runners are. She sees nothing but emaciated women. It does not take a detective to observe that the top Olympic female distance runners have incredibly low body fat. She then decides that this makes the difference between their abilities and her own. Alternatively, a hard-working endurance athlete may notice that she starts to run better or faster when she loses a little weight, perhaps initially as a factor of increased training volume rather than conscious dieting. Once she notices her performance improves with the weight decrease, she is filled with motivation to lose more. *If five pounds helped me improve my time by twenty seconds, imagine what fifteen pounds will do.* When losing weight reinforces that her times improve, an invested female runner is likely to continue down that path – even if she is already very thin.

It is simple physiology: the less body fat you carry, the faster you can run. Body fat does not contribute favorably to physical performance, whereas lean body mass (muscle, bone, water, tendons) does. The most elite female athletes carry just over what is known as essential body fat (the amount the body requires to have around the organs to cushion them). The paradigm of having the least amount of body fat possible and running performance

207

improvement is one of the unfortunate truths of the sport – and one, I believe, that when coupled with the personality similarities of great runners and anorexics, greatly contributes to the prevalence and severity of eating disorders in female distance runners.

61.
Helping People

As I MENTIONED, THE final push I needed to write this memoir came after I wrote a blog post on my website[1] in response to a *New York Times* article[4] about two young girls who participate in serious endurance events. The blog post was my first public admission of my eating disorder, and I discussed the challenges I faced then and now as a competitive runner. The reaction from friends, peers, former teammates, and people I did not even know was overwhelming: people were interested in what I had to say. Many comments supported my brave decision to post such a personal discussion, while others asked questions or shared stories of their own struggles. One girl who I met after college sent me the email below:

Hi Amber! How r u doing? U keep on running, right?

I read the article you wrote expressing your opinion about a competitive running at very young age. I admire you for your accomplishments as a runner and especially for defeating anorexia. I am writing this letter for you in a hope u could share with me your advices, ideas and best approaches me and my mom could use to help my sis who suffers from anorexia for over 7 yrs already. In your article you mentioned that while putting on pounds you were going thru lots of physical pain due to injuries etc and u also mentioned that you were going thru even bigger and stronger emotional distress. I am trying to understand my sis. However, me and my mom we have totally different approaches towards her. My mom's health is hit very hard by the stress over my sis's condition and weight. Whenever my mom comes with a visit to my sis or talks on a phone with her, my mom cries a lot and constantly is asking her to eat more carbs, proteins etc. My sis gets upset with her and doesn't enjoy her visits when that happens. Me, on the other hand, I'm talking with my sis about everything except the food and she enjoys my visits. My sis is very intelligent person but so stubborn too. It seems like she wanted to be so perfect in every direction and ended up on having to fight with this sickness. She has been a patient a Elmhurst Hospital for about 1 year and 4 months already. Mostly she was being mistreated while on medical floors. Now her treatment seems more reasonable. She has to drink 5 cans of Ensure daily and my mom left her job so she could bring her home cooked meals. However, most of the time my sis chooses to eat only fruits and vegetables. Oh it's so hard with her. She doesn't get any food therapy She constantly shows her concern about feeding me.

So I wanted to ask you if you think it's right that nobody really talks to her about food, except my mom. Is it good that my mom constantly begs her to eat more and cries and eventually upsets my sis? I feel like for me there is no need to talk about it coz I believe she knows what she gotta do to be discharged.

I will appreciate any advices I hear from. Thank you so much!! Hopefully I hear from you soon!

I responded:

Thanks for reaching out. I hope you've been doing well. I appreciate you opening up and sharing a very personal story and I'd be happy to offer my advice. I am certainly not a doctor or eating disorder therapist, but I do believe that having suffered with anorexia for so many years, I have some thoughts you may find useful.

First of all, I'm so sorry that your sister is suffering from the disease. It is brutal – both for her, and for you and your mom who love her. I can't imagine how painful it is to watch someone you love treat their body that way and not see the consequences. You guys must feel helpless. The good news, is there are things you can do that help.

The main thing to keep in mind is that most likely, your sister is not going to get healthy unless she wants to. You and your mom can say all the things you want to her to try and convince her to eat, but unless she wants to change and sees the damage she is doing, I think it does not have much effect. In that way, I think you have the right approach with her by not really mentioning food. Quite honestly, she probably really, really needs your love and companionship when you visit. You feel like an ally to her and she's probably cut most other friends out of her life. Anorexia is very isolating. I imagine you are a truly important person in her life. If she was not receiving hospital treatment, I would recommend that you should talk to her about food because perhaps she would listen, but I think since she is already under medical guidance, your most helpful role is just to love her and be her friend. This does not mean you should ever "enable" her eating disorder. Don't let her encourage you to help her get around eating more, have your mom stop bringing her food, etc. You should be the friend she needs, perhaps occasionally expressing your concern about how you wish you could help her recover. You are right – she knows what she needs to do to be discharged but she has to find it within her own heart and mind why she should start eating.

I think a mom's role is somewhat different. I am not a parent yet, but I think it's within a mom's blood to be concerned about the well being of her children. Your mom's instinct is to force the issue and get her to eat. After all, her health is in danger. In my struggles with the disease, I meant several people who passed away. Anorexia, as you know, is no joke. A mom cannot really sit on the sidelines so to speak, and let your sister go about her food aversions without trying to intervene. Because of that, we can't really ask or expect your mom to change. You may suggest to her that your sister is under medical care and there's not much benefit to nagging her. Explain to your mom that your sister needs to feel loved. Even though it is BECAUSE your mom loves your sister, she is trying to address the issue; anorexia is a mental disease that does not allow the inflicted person to think so rationally. She sees your mom as annoying and hating her because she is constantly upset with her. Your mom can bring food, encourage eating, but also sometimes try to be neutral and just have a stress-free visit, talking about other things.

My mom certainly nagged me and tried to force me to eat 24/7. I hated her for this and thought she hated me because the state of my health always made her cry and we were constantly fighting about my weight/diet. In hindsight, of course, I realize this was entirely out of love, but in the thick of things, we had a dreadful relationship.

My love to you and your family and please feel free to email me back with any other questions or thoughts and I can try to help. If not, I can always just be a friend if you want to talk. Your mom can also email me if she wants.

Take care,

Amber

62.
Kids Are Invincible

MY OPINION IS THAT children and adolescents do not have the same appreciation for life that adults do. Children feel invincible. Kids jump off playground equipment, sprint around without thinking that they could get hurt, and act without restraint. Likewise, I believe the feeling of invincibility is partly to blame in cases of teenagers driving too fast, binge drinking, doing drugs, and engaging in other risky behaviors. While these actions can be related to numerous factors including rebellion and peer pressure, some of it, I believe, also has to do with feeling like they aren't going to suffer any lasting consequences. It takes time for the ramifications of past choices to manifest in our bodies, especially when we are young, because young bodies fight tirelessly to keep us healthy, despite our mistreatment.

My coaches, parents, doctors, and medical specialists tried on numerous occasions to educate me on the consequences of the prolonged starvation that I was putting my body through. They cited wisdom such as, "you won't be able to run as well in college," "you'll be more susceptible to stress fractures," and "you'll want to be healthy and have a baby when you are an adult, and you are damaging your body now." Only now do I see that they were correct about each and every one of these predictions. At the time, none of that sage advice sunk in a meaningful way for me. The future was not something tangible; it was not something I could imagine. Plus, when adults told me I wouldn't be able to walk when I was eighty, I pictured my grandparents in their late seventies and thought, *they can't walk either. What's the difference?* The only future that felt important was the next race, maybe the next season – but certainly not ten, twenty, or sixty years down the road.

I was very lucky that despite all the running and caloric restriction, I did not incur a major injury until the stress fracture in my foot during cross-country season in my junior year of high school. I had minor, acute sprains and strains along the way, but fortunately they never amounted to much. I felt immune to the various risks of my anorexia that I was threatened with because I did not experience immediate setbacks, or could not picture the future possible consequences bothering me. One of the best ideas for coaches, mental health practitioners, and family members to help encourage recovery is to find a way to make the future feel more tangible and important.

63.
The Role of Coaches and Parents

EATING DISORDERS PLACE TREMENDOUS stress on relationships – between siblings, parents, family, coaches, teammates, teachers, peers, coworkers, and managers. Finding a way to mediate the situation is undoubtedly tricky. Coaches may be in one of the tougher roles, particularly those who head competitive high school or collegiate programs. They are expected to win, or at least that is the assumed goal. In order to achieve this, the coach wants to assemble the fastest team possible. More often than not, an anorexic runner is a fast runner – if not the fastest. This can be attributed to her low body fat (making her body more efficient at running quickly) and to her personality, which is probably one of intense discipline, a common trait among hardcore athletes. As long as the runner is healthy enough to run (and not sidelined with an injury), most coaches opt to allow her to compete. After all, she is usually leading the team to the fastest finish. In the college running scene, the entire varsity squad may be dominated by anorexic women. No coach is going to sit out his or her whole team.

Another challenge that a coach faces is simply determining whether the athlete has an eating disorder. By nature, fast female runners tend to be thin. Added to this genetic selection for skinnier women, distance running expends a significant amount of energy (calories), which can lead to a lean physique. The bigger issue is that one of the cornerstones of anorexia is denial of the issue. Like alcoholism, drug usage, or other addictions, anorexics deny that they have an eating disorder. Girls who suffer from anorexia are highly unlikely to admit to having the disease, so coaches essentially have to observe behaviors, try to get opinions and evidence from others who spend time with a girl in question, and then approach the athlete, accusing her of having the illness.

Most coaches, particularly at the high school level, only see the athletes during practice time – a maximum of two hours a day. Food is usually not involved during this time, so it is a rare occurrence for the coach to see their athletes eat (or not eat). Therefore, the coach can have a difficult time finding any concrete evidence of a suspected disease. Of course, there are physical signs, such as extremely low body weight, refusal to maintain a "normal" weight for height, dry hair and nails, and downy hair on the skin and face. There are also emotional clues including moodiness, fatigue, depression, irritability, or acting withdrawn.

Coaches sit between the ultimate rock and hard place: they want to keep their athlete running because she is competing well, but they need to keep her healthy to ensure success in future races. With that said, coaches can play the important role of a liaison between anorexic athletes and their teammates and family members. Other teammates are more likely to approach the coach if they suspect one of their peers has an eating disorder. Coaches may need to be the ones that approach the athlete and express concern. At the high school level, parents of an athlete with an eating disorder may be in close communication with the coach about their child's illness.

However, the most important role of the coach should be to educate his or her team. The coach should provide information to his or her athletes, as well as their parents, either directly or by inviting a sports nutritionist to work with the team. Information about the signs and symptoms of eating disorders, the risk of eating disorders in female athletes, as well as the long-term consequences of such illnesses, should be presented along with ideas about how to help loved ones, friends, and teammates who are suspected to have an issue. These sessions may be an appropriate time to establish ground rules that provide meaningful consequences to an athlete for allowing their eating disorder to continue untreated.

As I said for myself, hearing about long-term consequences meant nothing to me. I could not have cared less about that. I was concerned with my next big race and being better for that specific day. Perhaps if there had been rules that would have prevented me from running the upcoming race, I would have been more attuned to the consequences. Of course, these are difficult decisions for a coach to make.

Teammates need to have an environment that fosters open communication about the diseases. Because talking about eating disorders is taboo, it takes tremendous courage and concern to approach a teammate who you suspect has an eating disorder. More likely than not, this conversation will result in resistance, denial, defensiveness, and irritable behavior from the athlete. The same holds true for friends and peers, parents, and even coaches. While this might make it sound like confronting a friend or teammate would be pointless, my belief is that despite the high probability of the conversation going negatively, it is still impactful.

I was comfortable with my friends and teammates. No one said anything; people let me be. The people I did talk to about personal things never asked me if I was anorexic. I thought either they didn't know, couldn't tell, or it didn't bother them. While this was probably the case for some of my friends, I think more of them knew about the disease but didn't know what to do about it, or thought they couldn't make a difference. I think if I had more people "on my back" about my disease, I would have felt more uncomfortable in my skin, and that discomfort may have pushed me a little harder to get help.

As humans, we desire to be accepted by our friends. If we interpret that they aren't accepting us, we either ditch them (which I certainly did to some friends, to my regret) or try to fit in better, either consciously or subconsciously. Friends should not be enablers. While they don't have to continually force the issue, my thinking is that they may be the most likely group of people to have a favorable impact.

Most naturally, parents are going to be involved in the confrontation and treatment of the athlete. Unfortunately, this is not an easy position. I think the nature of the illness causes terrible rifts between parent and child, because the parent wants to "fix" the child and the child does not want to be fixed. The vast majority of anorexics do not want help. They are resigned to their life being the way it is. However, in the case of minors, parents have more control over the situation. My parents would forbid me from going certain places at times, competing in certain races or practices. They forced me to eat certain things and see my pediatrician three times per week. They enforced rules about weight gain, calories, and time spent running. While some of these rules were not directly successful, the fact that there were so many rules reminded me I was constantly being watched. My anorexia was an issue that my parents were not going to accept.

In many ways, my mom had no credibility to speak with me about my disorder, because she had an issue as well. This was infuriating to me as a teenager. How could she tell me to eat when she didn't? With most healthy parents, this should not be a factor. It's extremely important to stress that even teenagers, who are the epitome of rebellion, look to their parents for examples on a subconscious level. If you are a contradiction, you lose credibility.

Siblings are in the same challenging position that parents are, although it is one of even less authority. In my case, both my sisters wanted me to get better, and over the near-decade that I struggled with anorexia, they attempted to interact with me by encouraging, nagging, or insisting that I eat. I do not recall any of my extended family ever saying anything. One of my grandmothers once announced, "When she gets hungry enough, she'll eat." I say all of this to point out that most people follow the social norm that eating disorders, like other addictions, mental illnesses, and sometimes politics, are generally taboo topics.

64.
Looking Back

My mom sent me this email after reading my blog post[1] that inspired me to write this memoir:

I wish we could have a "do over" for those years and that somehow we could make it come out differently.

I wish that you could have a wide audience of young athletes to read your post, as well as the parents of those athletes. It is honest and since you are not that many years beyond the experiences it is very timely.

Those were such challenging years with you. You were, and are, so gifted in so many areas it was difficult to put brakes on you. You were being ravaged by such a terrible illness and despite what I felt were my best efforts, I didn't help you. I should have put you in the hospital, I should have stopped you from running. It seemed like an impossible conflict. I'm so very sorry you are suffering the consequences now.

It is brave for you to share the information and it also is evidence that you have healed in many ways. I'm sure you still struggle with the eating issue regularly but you seem to have pretty good control over it. Maybe you should try to get the blog or some form of it published?

I love you honey and I am so proud of where you are in your life now.

Mom

There wasn't a guidebook for my parents when I developed anorexia, and especially not one that dealt with what to do when your daughter is an elite athlete with anorexia. They did the best they could with the resources they had to try and balance the situation of loving their daughter, wanting her to be happy, and wanting her to be healthy. I think they believed that if they took away running, I would become so depressed that I would never get better, or worse, I would hurt or kill myself - I was that depressed.

I believe, to some degree, my parents also wanted me to continue succeeding in running. It improved my self-esteem, gave me friends, and opened doors for a funded college education, among other undeniable perks. Since they both enjoyed running on their own, I think it was fun for them to see me run so well. Parents love to have successful children; it reflects positively on them. If your child is doing great, you must be a fabulous parent. (Mine certainly were, but it had nothing to do with my fast race times.)

65.
My Parents

MY PARENTS WERE USUALLY on the same page with one another about how to handle my disease, treatment, running, and eating. But sometimes the stress of the situation and the seeming uniqueness of my case (I was an elite runner and doing better and better, after all), drove them to opposing sides. They would fight at night while I was upstairs in my bedroom. I'd tiptoe down the stairs and sit in the darkness, listening. Usually Mom would say she wanted me to run less or sit out a race or practice, or be subject to another "rule." Dad would say that as long as the weight stayed constant or I was "trying" to gain weight, I should be allowed to run. Of course, this dichotomy made me love Dad more, and my mom's "unsupportive" behavior rendered her the enemy.

Mom and Dad vacillated in their support of my running and hounding me to eat. I believe they were very proud of my dedication to the sport. They came to the majority of my high school meets, even when the races were far away. They both had their individual ways of cheering for me during races, and I knew how to listen for them, even in a big crowd.

I am not a parent yet, so I cannot honestly imagine the stress my eating disorder caused my parents. One interesting thing, which might not be very comparable (although ironic), is that my dog, Comet, went through a phase of starving herself. My husband and I adopted her when she was about five months old, and initially everything was going well. She was healthy, happy, loving, and easy-going, much like I was as a little girl. And, like all dogs, she loved to eat. Then we took her to get spayed. After the surgery, she decided that she was no longer going to eat.

Weeks went by. The war to get Comet to eat waged on. She was rapidly losing weight, and since she was supposed to be growing, that was problematic. We tried different brands of food. We sprinkled it with Parmesan cheese. We put in clumps of peanut butter, animal fat drizzled on top, or plain chicken. She wouldn't eat any of it. We heated and mashed the food. We tried giving her plain cheese. She refused it all. The veterinarian said to keep trying; she needed to eat, and there was nothing physically wrong with her. Eventually she was so skinny and desperately in need of calories that we literally sat on the floor with her and spoon-fed her every day. Comet would clench her jaw shut as if to say, "No way, Mom." We would pry her teeth apart and try to shove food in, and then force her to keep her mouth shut until she swallowed. Eventually she began eating normally. These were quite stressful times for me, and yet Comet is a dog. I can't imagine the stress and helplessness you must feel if your child won't eat.

My parents separated when I was in college, and after a few more rocky years, finally got divorced in 2010. I'm sure their relationship had issues much deeper than I was privy to, but I am quite certain, in the private darkness of my mind, that my issues exacerbated their problems.

66.
Current Running Philosophies

MY ATTITUDE TOWARD RUNNING these days has evolved significantly since my high school years. In my heyday, I would run come hell or high water. If I had an ache, I would run. If it was sleeting on an ice-blanketed street on a dark January morning, I would run. If I already ran that day, often I would still run. I wanted to be a professional runner; I wanted to be the best.

After years of injuries, months of hating running for what it made me do to myself, and years of frustration that I was "no longer fast," my philosophy and attitude toward running have shifted. I still love to run, and even enjoy racing periodically. The simple act of lacing up my shoes and heading out the door fills me with excitement and happiness. I'm not the type of runner that only relishes in the post-run euphoria. I genuinely enjoy the practice of running. If given the opportunity, I would still be a professional runner. Unfortunately, I recognize that goal is not attainable for me. The best I can hope for is to continue improving and try to get faster than I used to be, now within a healthier body.

I limit my mileage now. Part of that is logistical: as a working adult, the time devoted to running is limited compared to hours of practice as a young runner. Life gets in the way more – work, family, and other obligations take precedence.

For me, the other major part is that my body cannot endure routine high mileage training without incurring injuries. This may be because my bones were significantly weakened by the years of malnutrition during the important bone-building pubertal years. As a young runner, I was blessed with an injury-free, resilient body. Even though I pushed the limits of very high mileage, my body took the abuse without immediate consequence. This fortune was probably due to good biomechanics, luck, and the fact that I was only about seventy pounds at most while "pounding" the streets. My first injury was junior year of high school, even though I hit eighty miles per week a few times during sophomore year. Eighty miles is about twice the volume of most competitive high school girls' programs. Amherst was a high mileage school, but even our coach limited us to about fifty per week in the peak phase of base training during the summer. Most normal healthy weight, even robust females, cannot take eighty miles without injury.

The stress fracture in my foot that I sustained at the Great American Race also taught me to listen to my body and back off when I feel pain. Had I rested right after that race, I may have only needed a few weeks of non-weight-bearing exercise rather than a solid eight, with some weeks of part-time running and part-time cross training that followed. I would much rather run than cross train, so I usually find it safer to skip a run or cut one back when I notice pain so that only a few runs may be sacrificed, rather than weeks stuck in a gym cross training. Since that initial injury my junior year, I have incurred countless other physical setbacks – a half-dozen stress fractures, severe tendonitis in numerous parts of my body, muscle strains, and a back issue, just to name a few. I now know to listen more carefully to my body, rein myself in when need be, and wait until I am pain-free to push onward.

My goals are different now as well. I race far less often. In high school, small races occurred several times per week, and usually once every other week was an important race. In college, races were generally every Saturday, although I was so frequently injured that I rarely ran in them. Now I run a few races per year, depending on how healthy my body has been.

I used to run races to win. I was competing against a field in which I was certainly in the top few seeds. Road races that I now enter are co-ed; men are always faster than women, and therefore, I am never in the top handful overall. I live in New York City – a city of over eight million people, including many, many runners. Races draw tons of locals as well as travelers who come to run in the iconic city. Furthermore, many of the big-ticket races offer hefty prize purses. Even among women, it is rare that I am an overall winner—although in this past year, I have won two of the three races I entered (and got second in the other)! Even so, my goal is not usually to win. Rather, I generally have a finish time in mind.

I would occasionally set time goals when I was younger, but these were usually reserved for track races. Finish place was almost always more important to me. In fact, for some races my coaches would instruct me to run just fast enough to win, saving my energy for more competitive races. Also, in cross-country, because courses vary significantly in terms of terrain, ease, and condition, I often did not set time goals unless I had run the same course before. A 5k time on one cross-country course does not necessarily translate to the same time on another. Truthfully, the same is true with road races. Even if the distance is the same within two races, the course difficulty can vary widely. However, there are fewer markers of success, rendering finish time the most obvious goal.

67.
Unexpected Aftershocks

IT STILL FEELS UNNATURAL for me that I don't need to hide how much I do or don't run. Ben is incredibly supportive no matter what. Similarly, I don't have to hide how much I do or don't eat. It finally feels that my life is balanced and my relationships with food and exercise are appropriate.

I recently spoke to one of my fitness clients about my anorexic days. She has confessed that she also battled anorexia, but as an adult. One thing we both agreed on was that it's surprising that now our bodies will not allow us to slip back into restrictive eating patterns. Even just several hours of deprivation leads to inevitable, inescapable cravings for food. These cravings are so powerful, so inexorable, that we must comply and eat. As she said, "Even when I want to be anorexic again, my body won't let me."

68.
A Life Enriched

EVEN THOUGH RUNNING AT an elite level as a teenager encouraged me to lose so much of myself, I can't deny that it also provided me with some invaluable opportunities and opened many doors for me. I've traveled to places I would have otherwise never been able to see. I've met some of the best people in my life. I almost certainly got a leg up on college acceptances, and I was able to pay less for secondary education. I've been given opportunities for jobs. I won my honeymoon.

Running has enriched my life socially as well. Runners make up a unique, tight-knit family. Even when they don't know one another personally, they share a special bond. Many of my best friends have been runners. Running has given me mentors who have taught me about myself and about life, father figures when I needed them most, and introduced me to people I may have otherwise never met.

I am much more than a runner, but at the same time, running has been instrumental in shaping who I am today, as well as who I was at other stages of my life, for better or worse. Running has given me an outlet for my ADHD, which, if it were not as well controlled (thanks to running), would have gotten me in even more trouble than it did.

When I was thirteen, I was surfing the Adidas website one night before bed. I stumbled upon a contest that I decided to enter, without telling my parents. The challenge was to write a 500-word essay about "what makes an athlete an Olympian." It was the spring of 2000, just a few months before the Olympics in Sydney, Australia. I had been dreaming of being an Olympian since the day I strapped on my Tevas and ran around the neighborhood. The essay came together more naturally than any school assignment I ever had.

One paragraph read,

> If I were to become an Olympian, I would do whatever it would take. I would build up all the necessary strengths. I would train long and hard, work to my fullest potential, set seemingly impossible goals but work to make them possible, and dare to win. I would fight whatever was working against my strengths so that I could do whatever it was that I set my mind to do...My goal is to become an Olympian.

A few weeks later I received a congratulatory letter in the mail – I was one of the finalists in the essay contest! Eight boys and eight girls were flown to Sacramento, California, for the Outdoor Track & Field Olympic Trials. It was the first major prize for anything I had ever won, and it could not have been more exciting or better suited for me. I was thrilled at the opportunity to watch the Trials live. Plus, I was going to participate in a pentathlon in the stadium, competing against the other finalists for one of two coveted female tickets to watch the Olympic Games in Sydney.

There was one glaring problem: I was an, accomplished distance runner, but had no experience in most of the actual pentathlon events. I was even terrible at the ones I *did* know how to do. That didn't deter me. It was back in the days where I felt I could do anything I set my mind to. My positive attitude was unwavering, almost delusional at times. I believed I could do everything if I worked hard enough.

My mom took me to the high school track on a Saturday afternoon. I practiced sprinting 100m, and I ran and flew into the sand for long jump. And there by the sand pit we found our implement – a 16-pound shot put. The one I needed to use for the competition was only eight pounds, but this one was free (we eventually returned it) and I figured, the heavier the better. *I'll get even stronger and the light one will feel like a cinch.* Looking back, I realize it was about one-third of my weight! My mom had to help me hoist the shot put up to my shoulder. Then I "spun" around and released. It fell right to my feet. "I'm the bomb at this, Mom!" I exclaimed gleefully. Mom replied with a good dose of reality, "More like you bombed it, Am."

Then there was the "turbo jav," a training tool javelin throwers use to hone their skills. We used it in place of an official javelin, which, given my tiny size, was a very fortunate thing. We ordered a turbo jav online from a specialty track & field retailer. When it finally I arrived, I ripped open the box, read the directions and ran outside. I leapt around the front yard throwing the thing wildly, then chasing it, and throwing it again. I was like a kid with a butterfly net. I practiced all of these events for a few weeks, not making any real progress – but my confidence grew, which made me feel like I was improving.

When the trip finally came, I felt like a rock star. I flew all by myself to California, where I was greeted by one of the chaperones. Each finalist received a large Adidas duffle bag filled with running gear, some of which I still wear today. We met the rest of the finalists and learned more about our schedule for the upcoming few days.

The privilege to watch the professionals in my sport compete to realize their dreams was an invaluable experience for me. I was so inspired by their greatness.

As for the pentathlon, I fared okay, coming in third. I was so much smaller than my fellow contestants, even though we were all the same age. Although I did not make it to Sydney, there were many other things I "won" on that trip, and even at the time, I was proud of how well I did. I felt like a VIP at the trials, and thought that a shot at the Olympics was an attainable goal for me when I "grew up." I recently uncovered the essay nearly thirteen years after writing it. Interestingly enough, despite the writing being of rather poor quality, my sentiments are nearly the same today. One line said, "Some day...people will see me as a role model...and look at my picture and think to themselves, "She had the power to do it, so I can too."

Running undoubtedly helped me get admitted to some prestigious colleges. I was aggressively recruited, and my running successes certainly helped give me a leg up in all of the admissions processes, as well as in financial aid packages. Additionally, when I decided at the last minute that I wanted to attend UMass for my sophomore year rather than return to Duke, Coach Julie was willing to help me navigate the late admissions process and get me in. If I had not been a top-tier runner (and Julie hadn't been willing to put her neck on the line for me), this would not have been a possibility.

My résumé is bolstered by my participation in cross-country and track, particularly at the collegiate level. My list of running achievements makes me more attractive to employers and clients in the fitness industry, and gives me some credibility. These together have, I'm sure, given me a leg up in job acquisition. If you run for a collegiate team, particularly D1 (UMass was also D1, and I was a captain during my senior year), you must possess a certain drive, understand teamwork, be dependable, tough, and value hard work. Many employers know this and are more likely to take a chance on an athlete than someone with similar educational qualifications that lacks the team participation.

In June 2012, I ran the Portugal Day Five-Mile Road Race put on by New York Road Runners and the Portugal Tourism Association. I ended up getting second place in 29:52, which came with a lucrative seven-night trip for two to São Miguel Island in the Azores (Portuguese Islands in the Atlantic Ocean). The truth is, I was cold and extremely overwhelmed by the crowd at the post-race festivities, so I really wanted to leave. I knew I had come in second place, but I did not know that this finish came with such a luxurious prize. Ben said, "Am, let's stick it out a little longer for the awards ceremony. They are going to start soon." It is my style to run, cheer on people who finish after me, cool down a bit, and then head home to take the dog out and get on with the day.

I'm relieved I stayed because the trip included airfare for two and seven nights in a hotel in the capital city, Ponta Delgada, with breakfast and a whale watch. It was the first big prize that I had ever won, and more importantly (and surprisingly), I was completely healthy and eating plenty. The best thing about it was that it was going to be perfect timing: I was getting married that August to Ben, my best friend and biggest fan, and the trip made a perfect honeymoon.

Ben was my rock during the "fall from glory" from the distance running elite to the so-so crowd, while I watched others capturing the dreams I had once envisioned possible. He was a huge support when I dealt with injury upon injury and was stuck in a gym cross training, and when I felt worthless and lost my sense of self. Ben accompanied me to most of my post-collegiate road races after moving to New York City – even sticking it out for marathons and half marathons. He was there to console me when I ran poorly, he was there with warm clothes to meet me at the end, he was there to hail a cab when I was ready to speed home, and he was there to listen to me strategize training schedules and racing plans, or debate myself about which races to sign up for. It seemed like a perfect blessing that running had *finally* given me something I could give to him that we would not be able to do otherwise.

Ben and I do not have a lot of money. Living in New York City is expensive, and neither of us have lucrative careers. We had probably the lowest-cost wedding a Manhattan couple has ever had outside of City Hall. In fact, City Hall was our plan until about five weeks before the wedding, when we decided with my mom's help, we could take the ceremony to the park. We had a beautiful, casual Friday evening ceremony in August where we exchanged personal vows in front of our immediate families. Ben and I had originally discussed going camping for our honeymoon, or perhaps "splurging" for a cabin in the Poconos. As you can imagine, winning the trip to the Azores was a perfect gift falling into my hands. I felt beyond elated that I had won something that Ben could benefit from – that my running had paid off for him, too.

Our trip to the Azores was a wonderful honeymoon. Running there was incredibly difficult due to the layout of the city, lack of sidewalks, and ridiculous hills, but the rest of the trip was an experience we will always cherish: drives up through the morning mist to view crater lakes, a hike through hot springs, hours relaxing on the private balcony panoramic views of both the port and hilly countryside, and endless laughter shared with Ben. Ben was beyond grateful that my race performance afforded us the trip, and I was so proud that I ran a five-mile race under a six-minute pace for the first time since my thinnest days in high school. It had been years – both literally, and in the feeling that my anorexic days were drifting further into the past – since I had run that well. I was back, but this time I was healthy and happy.

69.
The Road Continues

WHILE I CERTAINLY FEEL that I have "beat" anorexia, not every day is easy. As most people with eating disorders will attest, the disease never completely goes away. Because I have incurred so many physical and emotional repercussions from anorexia, there are daily reminders about my past. Occasionally, I still long for the days of being a nationally ranked, record-breaking runner but most days I am thankful just to be alive and healthy.

My goals for this book were threefold: to look introspectively and face my past demons to come to a better understanding about my anorexia, to be honest about my past with my loved ones, and to help at least one young runner. My hope is to spark a dialogue somewhere about the pervasiveness and seriousness of eating disorders in distance running or athletics in general, breaking the silence on an issue we should all be working to prevent.

My overpowering emotions towards my disease are ones of regret, embarrassment, shame, and guilt. I feel terribly about everyone that I hurt, the lies that I told, and the pain I caused my family. I can't change my past, but luckily, many people have stuck by me and allowed me to grow into a better person.

Even today, although I know I am healthy, I feel very disappointed in myself. I believe there was an expectation that I was going to be a superstar and take the world by storm, that essentially I would be a champion in anything that I wanted to do. But now I feel like the ultimate letdown: just a fitness trainer, with very few friends, who has lost important people, and ruined her body. I've watched my peers become doctors, lawyers, teachers, engineers, and loving parents. Despite being thrilled with my marriage, relieved to have repaired my relationships with everyone in my family, I have not amounted to the woman I dreamed to be.

I had such a single-minded focus on becoming a world-class runner when I was young, but when that did not work out, I not only had a poor understanding of who I was and what else I wanted out of life, but I lost all confidence in myself and my ability to be a productive member of society. My heart pulled back the reins on any ambitions that entered my mind during college – medical school, biomedical engineering, and physical therapy – out of self-preservation. The fall from the dream I had been chasing since seventh grade was so incredibly painful that I could not let myself pursue something that truly excited me again. If I didn't have a big vision, I couldn't be a big failure. While I was a bright young girl with self-esteem grand enough to know I could do anything I set my mind to, I emerged from my eating disorder as a young woman who felt that she deserved nothing, could not achieve anything, and would always be a failure.

While it is very painful to admit this deep disappointment in myself, I am continually working on being more like the person I want to be and understanding that I am not defined by my past. In closing, my opinion is that we can't fully understand and effectively change things we don't talk about. It is my hope that all readers of this book will continue the conversation within their own communities.

References:

1. "Amber Sayer: Educated Fitness Professional." Available at: www.ambersayer.com
2. American Journal of Psychiatry, Vol. 152 (7), July 1995, p. 1073-1074, Sullivan, Patrick F.
3. Anderson SE, Dallal GE, Must A (April 2003). "Relative weight and race influence average age at menarche: results from two nationally representative surveys of US girls studied 25 years apart". *Pediatrics* **111** (4 Pt 1): 844–50. doi:10.1542/peds.111.4.844. PMID 12671122.
4. Bearak, Barry L. "Young Endurance Runners Draw Cheers and Concerns." *The New York Times* 4 Nov. 2012: SP1. *NYTimes.com* Web. 4 Nov. 2012. <http://www.nytimes.com/2012/11/04/sports/too-fast-too-soon-young-endurance-runners-draw-cheers-and-concerns.html>
5. *Diagnostic and Statistical Manual of Mental Disorders.* 4th ed. Washington, DC: APA; 1994.
6. Eating Disorders Online. "Anorexia Athletica." http://www.eatingdisordersonline.com/types/anorexia-athletica. Accessed 12/15/12.
7. The Free Dictionary by Farlex. "Anorexia Nervosa." http://medical-dictionary.thefreedictionary.com/anorexia+nervosa accessed 1/2/13.
8. Medscape Reference. "Pediatric Anorexia Nervosa." (http://emedicine.medscape.com/article/912187-overview#a0104) accessed 12/12/12.
9. R.M. Malina and C. Bouchard (1991); *Growth, Maturation, and Physical Activity*; Champaign, IL; Human Kinetics. 12

10. Steiger H, Richardson J, Schmitz N, et al. Association of trait-defined, eating-disorder sub-phenotypes with (biallelic and triallelic) 5HTTLPR variations. *J Psychiatr Res.* Sep 2009;43(13):1086-94.
11. Sungot-Borgen, J. Torstveit, M.K. (2004) Prevalence of ED in Elite Athletes is Higher than in the General Population. Clinical Journal of Sport Medicine, 14(1), 25-32.
12. The National Association of Anorexia and Associated Disorders. "Eating Disorder Statistics." http://www.anad.org/get-information/about-eating-disorders/eating-disorders-statistics/ accessed 11/30/12.
13. The Renfrew Center Foundation for Eating Disorders, "Eating Disorders 101 Guide: A Summary of Issues, Statistics and Resources," 2003.
14. Wikipedia. "Hypergymnasia." http://en.wikipedia.org/wiki/Hypergymnasia. Accessed 1/2/13.

CPSIA information can be obtained at www.ICGtesting.com
Printed in the USA
LVOW13s0848191013

357675LV00001B/217/P